CH00688049

# 5 Numbers of Destiny

## CHANGE YOUR FATE - USING THE LOST ART OF ANCIENT CHALDEAN NUMEROLOGY

## Anmarie Uber

Tuggle Publishing
Fort Wayne, IN

Copyright © 2015 by Anmarie Uber.

Library of Congress Control Number: 2016905725
All rights reserved. No part of this publication may be reproduced, distributed or transmitted in any form or by any means, including photocopying, recording, or other electronic or mechanical methods, without the prior written permission of the publisher, except in the case of brief quotations embodied in critical reviews and certain other noncommercial uses permitted by copyright law. For permission requests, write to the publisher, addressed "Attention: Permissions Coordinator," at the address below.

Tuggle Publishing
P.O. Box 8166
Fort Wayne, IN/United States 46808-8166
www.tugglepublishing.com

Cover Design by Juliette at Silky Cover Design
Book Layout ©2013 Book Design Templates.com

Ordering Information:
Quantity sales. Special discounts are available on quantity purchases by corporations, associations, and others. For details, contact the "Special Sales Department" at the address above.

5 Numbers of Destiny/Anmarie Uber —1st ed.
ISBN 978-0-9974722-3-3

Tarot Card images by Anmarie Uber

# Contents

*Dedicated to:* My father Paul, who is with me in Spirit, my mother Sally, my siblings: Bob, Jean, Mary, Karla, John and Angela; Deborah Lee Taylor; my many beloved clients; friends; and Andrew Tuggle.

*Special Acknowledgments to those who helped bring this book into existence:* Many thanks to Juliette of Silky Cover Design for the fantastic cover, Chris Beck and Kathy Minnich for all of their help and friendship, Andrew Tuggle and Deborah Lee Taylor for their ongoing encouragement, support and unconditional love. For financial contributions: Angela Ueber (also helping to promote), Mary and Bill Seltenright, Brittany and Grant Seltenright, Joshua, Tiffany and Arlo Seltenright, Karla Ueber, Robin LeMesurier, Jonathan Buono, Larry B. Newman, Michael Moore, Christy Beauchot-Smith, Jon Hartman, Amy Wilson Brewer, Raquel Delagana, Joe Henry and Hasalyn Modine.

We do nothing alone.

*"One cannot escape numbers. Even zero is a number."*

—ANMARIE UBER

# Searching for Answers

My life was cursed. I knew it, and my astrology chart was confirming the bad news. It seemed I was fated to a life of challenges in partnerships, health issues and finances. I had to find an answer to my ongoing problems, which encompassed just about every major area of my life. There's nothing like having continual setbacks to motivate a person to find a way to change things, and so began my travels into the mysterious world of Chaldean Numerology.

I immersed myself into the study of astrology, palmistry, tarot and other related subjects, "trying on" the beliefs and principles of many spiritual paths. In the late 80's, I was simultaneously introduced to both the Pythagorean and Chaldean number systems. Although I had interest in, and studied each of these methods, I was drawn in by Chaldean, with its mystical prophetism, and its focus on fate, karma, and luck. I felt Chaldean Numerology was the answer to changing my reality.  What I did not realize back then, was that all the rules were not spelled out for me, and I would have to experiment *a lot.*  Being a true guinea pig, I signed myself up, along with friends, family and clients, who wittingly and unwittingly, joined in the study over the years. I examined the numbers of everyone and anyone, searching for patterns. I frequently changed my name, orchestrated events on certain days, chose partners, associates, addresses and towns (I moved a lot) according to numbers, and used various suggested methods of luck enhancement, with sometimes disastrous results, in all of the above.

Twenty-five years later, I decided it was time to write it all down, and formulate it.  This book has been a redefining of what little we know of Chaldean Numerology, into a system that not only works, but is expanded on in the areas of rules and calculation.  It has been simplified for anyone to understand. My journey has been an interesting, and at times painful one. One of the best ways of finding real answers, though, is through experience, and so you could say I lived this numerology book into existence. I hope you find the information helpful, and I hope it massively transforms your life for the better, as it has mine. God bless.  Anmarie

# Living in the Matrix

For me, the world is like a dream of the mind, in a constant state of change, and can therefore, never ultimately be relied upon to hold all of our answers. Science proves this, identifying the world as lacking real substance and made up entirely of energy, a holographic matrix. Even in a dream, though, there are many pathways, maps and guides to help you find your way. Some of these may lead you astray, some prove reliable, but none is more right or wrong than any other, in a dream. Life is an individual experience, and what is necessary or helpful to one person, may not be for another. Numerology is the same. There are many number systems, and all have value and purpose. I believe these numerology systems are one form of life's maps or guides, to help you create better circumstances for yourself Because your perception can change your reality, this world would have to be in a constant state of change, which eventually leads to chaos, or as I call it, *The Law of Chaos*. God (or the Creator/Central Source if you prefer), is the only true constant. God's *Law of Grace* is what raises us up out of our illusions, into happier outcomes; into joy and peace. Numerology helps get us a step closer to accepting this Grace, and avoiding the suffering of the world. It is the ego's belief that we need to suffer and sacrifice. When we decide to look at our numbers, we are seeking a higher path of joy; a joy which is the equivalent to the Godly State of Being, and a softening of the painful experiences.

There is more than one thought system, on how Chaldean Numerology should be calculated. I have taken the basic Chaldean number system and their age-old meanings, a few steps further, backing up my findings with patterns of conclusive repetitions, based on studying the lives of others. There are many other forms of numerology being practiced, today, that have different methods for calculating, because they are used for different purposes.

Chaldean Numerology has not been something one could find on mainstream bookshelves, as there have been very few books written about this number system. There are plenty of numerology books available, but for years, the large majority of these were based on a western interpretation of Pythagorean Numerology. This is a totally different system, and I want to stress here that these two systems of numbers, Pythagorean and Chaldean, have different purposes, and therefore should not be mixed together. I see a lot of people taking what little information is available on Chaldean numbers, and substituting the Pythagorean rules to compensate or fill in the empty blanks. This does not work, as you would be creating a whole new number system, that would need to be tested on its own. A good example of this, is someone adding their whole birth date together, to get the Pythagorean "Life Path Number", and reading the Chaldean meanings for that number. For one thing, this particular form of Chaldean Numerology does not add the entire birth date together, to arrive at one of the personal numbers. If you have a "Life Path Number of 9" in Pythagorean, it means that you are a humanitarian type of person, and this is your style of relating, as well as your motivation in life. "Nine" in Chaldean, however, means someone who is prone to having a temper, and would be dealing with war-like situations. The Chaldean nine is based on the day of birth, and connected to the qualities of the planet Mars.

Another good example of someone attempting to merge these two systems, is carrying over Master Numbers (11, 22, 33, 44) from Pythagorean to Chaldean. Some have been using the Pythagorean rule, that a master number should not be reduced, when calculating in Chaldean. There are no master numbers in this form of Chaldean, and not reducing them in certain calculations, causes you to come up with a number outcome that is misleading or incorrect. Master Numbers relate to a person's character development in Pythagorean, whereas the 11, 22, 33 and 44 are reduced in Chaldean calculations as needed, to find the predictive fate of the person. (I am not disagreeing with anyone who includes "master numbers" in studying *other* forms of Chaldean, or new versions of numerology, that they themselves have tested.)

There are many "Chaldean Numerology" sites on the internet today, that are missing the key elements in their calculations, that make this system work. For example, one cannot say, "I changed your name to a "23", which is a *very fortunate* number, and your life is going to be wonderful now." There is more to the story, for it to create enough of a change, to actually turn the person's life around (one has to look at how all the numbers interact with one another). In some cases, the individual's life gets worse. I know. I have experimented on myself many times, with name changes. Add to that, the Hidden Number is all but ignored, in these numerology calculations, as are the individual rules for each number. Therefore, I will endeavor to address and simplify these missed steps, so that it may advantage the many seeking assistance and a bettering of their life, from this number system.

## The differences:

Chaldean vs. Pythagorean:

| | |
|---|---|
| Based on astrology | Based on mathematical model |
| Day of birth is the major signifier | Birthdate is the major signifier |
| Day, month, year used separately | Adds together birth date |
| Does not use "master numbers" | Uses "master numbers" |
| Defines numbers 1-52 | Defines 0-9 |
| "9" is not a letter value | Uses sequential alphabet values |
| Compound numbers | Vowel/Consonant calculations |
| Determines fate, karma and luck | Analyzes character/motivations |

As can be seen, these are two completely different systems. There are also a lot of differences in Hindu, Gematria, "phonetic" Chaldean etc.

## Who are the Chaldeans?

There are many theories about this mysterious group of people, and differing versions of their history and teachings.

Some has been   preserved by modern-day Brahmins. The Chaldeans lived for a time in an area southeast of Babylonia, towards the coast of the Persian Gulf, on the right bank of the Euphrates. They arrived around 1000 BC. In Assyrian, the name was "Kaldu". The Chaldeans were not native to Mesopotamia, but rather, migrated from India. They were not Arameans, but Brahmanical Hindus (now called Aryans). When they ruled all of southern Mesopotamia, for a short time, "Babylonia" became synonymous, (mostly with the Greeks and Jews), with "Chaldean," but the Chaldeans were not Babylonians. The Chaldeans spoke a West Semitic language, but eventually adopted the Babylonian dialect of Akkadian, which was, for the most part the same, with the exception of slight differences in phonetics and characters. [1] These ancient peoples were known as astrologers or star worshipers, and were far ahead of modern times in their mathematical calculations, and grasp of astronomy, astrology, philosophy, architecture, numerology, divining and magic. The Chaldeans believed in one deity, but revered the Sun, Moon and other celestial bodies, as symbols of that deity. The Egyptians, Hebrews, Assyrians and Greeks learned the Chaldean sciences.

Supposedly Sabeanism was the religion of the ancient Chaldeans, but its principles are misinterpreted, and cannot be grasped or studied, as they are lost. The Chaldean Book of Numbers or "Book of Dzyan", and other writings, are in Arabic, their knowledge guarded by specific Sufi initiates. [2] It is believed that Chaldeans recognized and denounced the dark side, or what would be known as "fallen angels". Or this is

---

[1] Jewish Encyclopedia 1901-1905
[2] The Chaldean Legend, Ganino.com

what we surmise, from ancient Jewish mysticism and the knowledge of the use of amulets and symbols, being worn to ward off demons. The Chaldeans honored a Sabbath day of rest, as well as other days, reserved for prayer and gratitude. The number seven was considered sacred.

Chaldeans seem to be connected to alchemy as well, being considered the oldest known "magicians". They believed, that true power of magic, came from the power of the soul, and the knowledge of the alchemical or magical properties of plants, minerals and animals. They were able to contact higher spiritual beings, using the psychic senses, religious rites and prayer. To the Chaldeans, control of the physical world was merely scientific, accomplished by observing the natural laws. This knowledge made their feats appear as "miracles" or magic, to others. These were ancient scientists, and they were brilliant. The wisdom and practice of ancient scientists, had one natural philosophy in common that they followed, and that was to observe with their senses. They based facts on what made sense on every level of the universe, not just the physical.

The following is becoming common knowledge, but I find it interesting that in the Hebrew Bible, Abraham, the founding father of the Jewish religion, came from "Ur of the Chaldeans". (In Bactria there was a Jewish nation named Jaguda, or Ur-Jaguda. Ur meant "place or town".) It is also interesting, that other philosophic writers of Jewish history agree, and name Abraham as a teacher of science and astrology:

● Tomas Doreste, who in his book "Moises y los Extraterrestres", writes that the philosopher Voltaire believed Abraham to be descended from Brahman priests who had left India, and shared their teachings throughout Persia, to the lands near the Tigris and Euphrates. Voltaire noted that the city of Ur was near the border of Persia, the road to India where Brahma had been born. (Midway on this road is Bactria, a mountainous area where Brahma was said to be from.) "Chaldean" or "Kaul-Deva" (Holy Kauls) was the title of an ancient Hindu priestly caste of Brahmins.

- Philo of Alexandria, a Hellenistic Jewish philosopher from ancient Egypt, in the time of the Roman Empire had this to say in his doctrine *On Abraham*, "The Chaldeans exercised themselves most especially with astronomy, and attributed all things to the movement of the stars, believing that whatever is in the world is governed by forces encompassed in numbers and numerical proportions...seeking out the numerical arrangement according to the cycles of the Sun and Moon, the planets, and the fixed stars...."

- An ancient Jewish writer Eupolemus, (150 B.C.) writes that Abraham was trained in astrology, emigrated from Chaldea to Phoenicia, and taught the Phoenicians. Abraham also lived with, and taught the Egyptian priests at Heliopolis, and is descended from the "race of giants". According to Eupolemus, Abraham is glorified as the father of all science.

- The Jewish historian Artapanus of Alexandria, an Egyptian, wrote "Concerning the Jews," (250 - 100 BC). In this historical work, which was written in Greek, the three Jewish patriarchs Abraham, Joseph and Moses were responsible for altering the culture of the Near East.

Abraham, in particular, taught the Egyptian Pharaoh Pharothothes the science of astrology.

- Flavius Josephus, a Jewish scholar and historian, mentions in his book "The Antiquities of the Jews", that Abraham taught science to the Egyptians, who in turn taught the Greeks.

## Why Does Numerology Work?

Believing in numerology is an act of faith. Science can prove how numbers measure, but cannot prove why numbers seem to affect us. The belief in the efficacy of numerology, is in the seeing of patterns over and over. It is in the experience of using it, that belief and confidence in the system is found. Science can prove a lot of things, such as gravity. If a tree branch breaks off, it will hit the ground. Science, however, cannot tell you if the tree branch, that hangs over the room you currently sit in, is going to break and come through the roof. It is an act of faith that you sit there. It is an act of faith, every time you make plans for tomorrow, and go to bed. Science cannot tell you if you are going to die in your sleep, and if there will be a tomorrow. Therefore, science has its place, as do the things that are outside its parameters. Life, then, is an act of faith. So, you may never be able to fully understand why numerology works, but following its patterns, and your experiences with it, will show that it does. Numerology reminds me of psychology. The latter is considered a science, but it is really just a noticing of patterns of behavior. It is not a proven factual system. Numerology, like psychology, is the study of how numbers affect our behavior and future experiences, only "proven" by observation and reaffirmation, of its reliable consistency. If you approached the idea that numbers have an effect on your life, from a scientific viewpoint, you would say that everything is made up of numbers in its very nature, form, organization and structure. Therefore, numbers rule your world. You cannot set your alarm, buy a car, pay a bill, watch TV, call a friend or any "number" of other things, without numbers. Your world is measured and run by magical digits.

The ancient Chaldeans discovered an agreement between the seasons and certain fixed stars. Thus began their belief, that the Earth and heaven were interrelated, and ran in cycles. They studied and documented the numerical patterns of the stars and planets, and noted their effects on our lives. These cosmic bodies magnetically affect you, just as the moon's tides, solar flares and sunspots cause changes in the earth's atmosphere and weather. (Or is it us, affecting them?)

Numbers, in numerology, relate to the energy of your name and birth date. Your personal numbers are connected to the planets in our solar system, including the Sun and Moon. We know that energy matter is made up of atoms, which contain electrons or protons. These electrons and protons have magnetic charges of positive or negative, just like a battery. Your human cells are magnets. You have an electrical body and brain waves, measured in terms of electromagnetic energy frequencies. Your emotions are electromagnetic energy, and are vibrating at a certain magnetic frequency level. This is why your thoughts or moods can repel or attract another person. Others can feel or sense the mood or emotions you are projecting. Because you are a magnet, the magnetic charge of the Sun's solar flares would naturally, then, affect you, as well as the Earth. Everything is magnetics, and everything happens in a numerological order that can be mapped and logged with numbers. So, numerology is a study of these planetary number energies, and their affect on human life.

There is a new cosmology on "plasma", which is considered a newly discovered element (solid, liquid, gas, plasma). It is believed to make up   99.99% of the entire universe, visible and invisible.  Plasma in space is a mixture of hot charged particles - ions and electrons, generating a lot of energy. It is only when it is cooled down that plasma becomes a solid, liquid or gas we would see on Earth. We have learned to function with, and utilize these lower states of slowed down magnetic particles.  In space, plasmas remain electrically charged, and respond more to electromagnetic forces than to gravity. "Empty" space is alive with a constant flow of plasma. Large bodies in space are believed to be interacting through magnetics, which is much stronger than gravity. In other words, planetary bodies appear to be "moving" based on whether they are attracting or repelling.  Anyone can see this dominance of magnetics over gravity by using simple magnets. Plasma waves are traveling at an unlimited velocity, not as transverse waves of light. They are longitudinal waves, and therefore not limited to the speed of light.  Plasma needs an electric current to run on. [3]

Think about the fact that your thoughts are electrically charged protein molecules. Your blood flow is an electrical current system. Every cell in your body is a pulsating electrical entity. All of it regulated, and measurable by numbers. I will leave it here for you to think deeper, on the planetary magnetic connections to you, their connections to number

---

[3] *Plasma (Physics).* (July 8, 2015). Wikipedia.

patterns, and their ultimate influence on your life. It is through study and experience, that one begins to believe that the effects are measurable and real. Remember Morphic Resonance?[4] Everything is by habit, thus creating pattern, and thus measurable by numbers...and changeable...

## Changing My Name

As I said before, I felt my life was cursed. We all have our difficulties. I was stuck, for years, in a pattern of attracting emotionally abusive relationships with men. They were addicted to either alcohol or drugs, and were financial vampires. Because of this, I struggled with money, almost my whole adult life. I became a workaholic by necessity, with little or no vacations. Add to that, my health was a constant challenge, forcing me to give up many pleasure foods, follow strict dietary habits and find alternative ways to heal myself. Also, strange circumstances frequently seemed to happen to me, to single me out. I remember in my high school yearbook, my picture was the only one without a name next to it. Senior year, my name was not on the voting list for prom court. Although enough people had penciled me in, to qualify me being on the court, student council suggested a re-vote. I thought it would be too embarrassing, so I declined. As I grew older, and continued to be singled out in many strange ways, I began to feel as if I something was wrong with me, and imagined that maybe I did not actually exist!

---

[4] Carroll, Rober Todd. (1994). *Morphic Resonance*. The Skeptic's Dictionary.

In an effort to change my patterns and circumstances, I turned to Chaldean Numerology. Because I had what I considered unlucky numbers, I started experimenting with changing my name. I used completely different names, and versions of my own name, altering the spelling. I found that my luck did not improve, but rather got worse. I eventually noticed patterns, and realized there were specific rules that had to be followed. One of the versions of my name was a "twelve", the number of sacrifice. Years of feeling the effects of the "sacrifice", led me to eventually come to a crisis point and realization. The twelve magnetically led me to move to a town, which added to the number "12", hence doubling its effect. Then everything became twelve. Membership numbers added to twelve, my address number, the apartment number, the time displayed on the clock, my change due at the store, credit card numbers, pet names...all twelves. The number continued to follow me. Anything I tried to accomplish in this twelve town was jinxed or wrecked, including an engagement to a fiance. It was time to sacrifice this name, or become the sacrifice.

In late fall of 2013, I decided to again change the name I was using, determined that it be the last time. I wanted to keep some semblance of my birth name, but this proved to be more difficult than I had anticipated. (Sometimes no version of a person's birth name will work.) I settled on "Anmarie Uber", the only spelling that would harmonize with my birth number, and create luckier numbers. (Privately, I still use the previous version of my name, *and the influence of both is felt in my life.*) The results have been astonishing. Even though the old spelling continues to curse me, "Anmarie Uber" has brought in many new blessings.

I used the new name for the first time, as an instructor of a workshop. That day I met my Twin Flame. He took my class, and we found that we had a very special spiritual connection. I attributed our meeting to my name change. My career life shifted, quickly and radically, as well, with opportunities to teach even more classes, and write this book. Media coverage showed up out of nowhere. People were finding me, and I was suddenly, no longer invisible to my good fortune. Life was noticing me. It was as if many obstacles had been removed from my path. In a month's time, of changing my name, I began regularly blogging, my online audience tripled, and I got offered to speak on two radio shows. My classes were getting booked out. So, I want to say here, that I don't agree with those who believe it takes a long time to see changes, after altering one's name. If it is done correctly, these will be positive changes.

This book will teach you how Chaldean Numerology is connected with Astrology. Each root number is assigned to a planet in our solar system, and has a magnetic affect on our future. You will benefit, from my years spent, testing the rules, looking for patterns, teaching this course, and evolving the system into a simplified model, that anyone can understand, and utilize to improve their life. You, too, can learn how to use Chaldean Numerology, to show you what fate has in store for you, and what you can do about changing that fate. I leave you now, to discover your destiny numbers...

# CHAPTER ONE

# 5 Numbers that Determine Destiny

How much did you pay for this book? How many pages are in it? You need numbers to answer these questions. Everything in our world, our bodies, nature and the entire cosmos, is made up of mathematical equations of numbers, utilizing the root numbers 1- 9. We do not know the origin of numbers, yet numbers tell us what day it is, where we live, what time we need to be at work, how many bones are in our body, and the measure of the gravitation, mass and speed of light, that determines the size of a black hole in outer space! All of life can, amazingly enough, be measured with combinations of *just nine numbers.*

These nine root numbers recur, in a sequence that repeats itself, with the use of the zero, determining the next series of numbers:

1 - 9

10 (1+0) =1

11 (1+1) =2

12 (1+2) =3

13 (1+3) = 4 ; and so on.

*It is amazing to think, that combinations of just nine root numbers and zero, will allow us to count up to infinity and beyond.*

## Your 5 Destiny Numbers

There are five numbers, in particular, that can open or close doors, attract lucky or unlucky circumstances, and create or remove obstacles to your success and happiness. These are derived from your birth date and name. They are simple to calculate, and act as a snapshot or blueprint of your life, setting the stage for what type of luck you are likely to experience, along the way. I call these five your Destiny Numbers. Destiny Numbers represent the outer workings of fate acting on your life. They are indicators of major events at some point in the future, and determine the amount of success an individual experiences. In some cases the Destiny Numbers reveal the manner in which you may die. I think everyone's life, in some area, feels a little out of control. Sometimes all of it seems out of control. The good news is, it is simple to alter unlucky destiny numbers to a more positive vibration. You can empower your life, by getting familiar with these five numbers, creating a flow that will eventually overcome or reduce obstacles, heartache and lack... none of which are your birthright. The Destiny Numbers are as follows:

● **THE DAY NUMBER**

The first Destiny Number is derived from the day you were born. It may be a single or compound (double) number. It is called the "Day Number".

An example: If you were born on Dec. 2, your Day Number is "2", a single digit. If you were born on Dec. 20th, your Day Number is "20", a "compound" or "double" number (but it also breaks down to a "2", because (2+0=2)). The numbers "2" and "20" are both "2s", butl each have their own meanings. Both will have a strong influence on your life.

*The Day Number is one of the most important numbers,* because it cannot be altered, and therefore must harmonize with the other destiny numbers. An individual cannot change the day on which they were born, so in essence they came into this life with the Day Number, and have to play out its influence. For this reason, it is said to reflect karma, accumulated from past lives. This could represent beneficial rewards, or unresolved negative lessons. The Day Number will give you certain personality tendencies, or propensities toward certain experiences. *It is how others see you, what type of material is attracted to you, or what can happen to you in life.* I will discuss your Day Number in more depth in the next chapter.

● **THE INDIVIDUAL NAME NUMBER(S) (INN)**

Each letter of the alphabet has a numeric value assigned to it, and the INNs are found by separately adding together the letters in your first name, last name, and/or any other names used in how you are addressed, such as a middle name, an initial or titles, such as "Reverend." An INN is the sum total of each name, and it is more common to have at least two or more, as most people use a first and last name. Each name number total, by itself, has an influence on your life. If one is commonly known by only a single INN, such as "Cher", "Shakira", or "Madonna", then there would only be one Individual Name Number (INN).

The name used for calculating your "Individual Name Number(s)" (INN), is the name you use the most, or how you are most commonly addressed by others. This includes nicknames. If you are almost always known by, and use a first and last name, you will calculate two INNs. If you are always called by a first, middle *and* last name, you will calculate three INNs.

*This number is important, because it is the only one you can change, in turn, altering the vibration of the other numbers.*

### ● THE TOTAL NAME NUMBER (TNN)

The "Total Name Number" (TNN) is the sum total of all the Individual Name Numbers (INNs). You add the first name INN total to the last name INN total, to find the TNN. (Note: The INN and TNN are not set in stone, and can be altered by the changing of one's name. This would be an option, if one had unfortunate numbers, and wanted to change their influence. There are specific rules for this, that must be followed, and will be addressed later in this book.) *It is very important that the TNN be in harmony with the Day Number* (see "Natural Harmonies" in this chapter). In Chapter Three, you will learn more about calculating your name numbers.

## ● THE HIDDEN NUMBER

The "Hidden Number" is found, by adding the Total Name Number (TNN) to the Day Number. Like the other destiny numbers, the Hidden Number represents a fate that will befall a person. It is a hidden fate that we are unaware of, until we add the Day and TNN together. The Hidden Number is often ignored, when choosing a different name, or calculating numbers, and can lead to unfortunate circumstances in one's future. There are specific rules to follow with this as well, and these will be addressed in Chapter Four.

## ● THE PERIOD NUMBER

The "Period Number" is based on a certain time period in which you were born. It relates to astrology Sun signs. If you were born in late April, or the first three quarters of May, you are a "Taurus". This time period of Taurus has the number "6" assigned to it. Therefore, if you are a Taurus, your "Period Number" is 6. Like the Day Number, *the Period Number cannot be altered*, but it can help enhance the positive qualities of your other numbers, and be used to harmonize otherwise negative numbers. (More on Period Numbers in Chapter Five.)

# CHAPTER TWO

# The Day Number

You were born with your own lessons to learn, whether that be through karmic reward or debt. (Your past lives determine the number of the day you will be born on, and what that karma will be.) I call the day of birth, the "Day Number". It is a very personal number for you, and will be with you all of your life. The Day Number sets up the type of energy or pattern of life you are set to live under, as payment or reward from previous karma, you brought into this life. It may reflect how others view you, and the type of circumstances you will encounter along your path. *Since this number cannot be changed, it is very important to have all of your other destiny numbers in harmony with this one*, if at all possible. This will bring luck, to help soften any difficult karma with this number, as well as enhance its good qualities, bringing an overall harmony to your life. (An unlucky Day Number's influence is altered, by enhancing the vibrations of the other destiny numbers...more on this in later chapters).

## Calculating Your Day Number

The Day Number is the easiest of the destiny numbers to calculate, as it is simply the day of your birth. If you are born on the 5th of any month, your Day Number is "5". If born on the 30th of the month, your Day number is the "double" or "compound" number "30". Thirty is also the "root" or "single" number "3" (found by adding 3+0=3). We can write this as "Day Number 30/3". If your Day Number is any of the single digits 1-9, read its meaning in the next section on "Meanings of Single Root Numbers". If it is a compound number of 10-31, first reduce it to its root number, and read the single number meaning. Next, read its compound number meaning, to determine fate's influence on your day of birth.

Examples:

Jean is born on October 4, 1961. Her Day Number would be a single "4".

Mary is born on May 18, 1980. Her Day number is compound "18" and a single "9" (1+8=9), or 18/9.

Following are the descriptions for single and compound numbers. I feel that these numerical meanings are not just descriptions, but rather contain literal predictive symbolism about future events. You will begin to see for yourself, how the future can show up in a very specific way, through the examples given in this book, and in the lives of those you know.

These single (root) and compound (double) numbers describe you, and what happens to you in this life. The single numbers describe characteristics and traits, of the astrology planet connected to your root number, how others may see you, and how these qualities affect your life experience. Single numbers deal with aspects of your physical and material world. They are the overall energy pattern or blueprint of your life. The compound numbers (10 - 52) represent outside forces of fate acting on you. These forces are hidden, and act in the background of the outer life, family, career, relationships and reputation, foreshadowing the future. They bring about specific circumstances, based on *the interaction of all your destiny numbers together* (just like hot water is not soup until you add all the ingredients, together creating a certain combination of flavors).

The Chaldeans are the creators of our week, Sunday - Saturday. The 52 numbers in this system, relate to the 52 weeks in a year. Your Day Number can only be one of the numbers 1-31, as related to the days in a month. (The meanings of the single and compound numbers will apply to your name, Hidden and Period Numbers, as well.)

Note: I believe the Major Arcana tarot cards followed the 52 Chaldean numbers, however, we only have 22 of these trumps in modern decks. I have designed my own picture interpretations of the 22 trumps, and given commentary on their meanings.

## Meanings of Single Root Numbers

1 Number one is ruled by the Sun, and represents all that is created and manifest. The basis of all life is one. One is a number of action and adventure, rather than contemplation. Those born on a one day are unique, and have originality.

They seek greatness, and are determined to have their individuality acknowledged. They are very creative and imaginative. There is no limit to these qualities. They aim for the top, and usually find themselves very high up the professional ladder, or at the top of their chosen field. They are good as authority figures, but still respect those under their rule. People look up to them. Ones storm ahead toward their ambitions, sometimes before thinking them through. They dislike restraint of any kind. Learning patience and perseverance, will help get them where they want to be. Ones should also cultivate inner peace, or anger could become their worst enemy, destroying the one's plans. A one person's drive is toward greatness, rather than the accumulation of wealth. It may be for the aggrandizement of themselves, or for the betterment of the world as a whole. For this reason, they may not end up wildly successful in the material sense, or may have a tendency to overspend. They do retain an ability to be practical, though, so the attainment of wealth is always a possibility, if they work to contain their anger, as mentioned above, and focus on diligence and patience.

This is a strong, regal number. Ones speak their minds openly, but others respect them, because they sense their inherent nobility and strength. Ones may be interested in the paranormal, and are usually politically active or informed. If born when the Sun is in exaltation - the period of the Vernal Equinox (March 21 - April 28) or during the "House of the Sun" (July 21 - August 28) , a political career could become a reality, as these are powerful time periods for number ones. Ones should take care of their health, at ages in the one series of numbers: 19, 28, 37, 55, 64, 73 and 82. Ones are compatible with the numbers 1, 2, 4 and 7.

A "1" individual should determine whether the number "4"

is bringing in a positive or negative influence in their life, before deciding to include this number in their personal numbers.

**Make Plans:** On "1" days (1st, 10th, 19th, 28th), especially during the Cancer number 2-7 period and the Leo number 1-4 period (6/21 - 8/20). Secondary are "2", "4" and "7" days.

**Lucky Days:** Sunday and Monday, especially if a 1, 2, 4 or 7 falls on that day.

**Lucky Colors:** All shades of gold, yellow, bronze and golden brown.

**Lucky Stones:** Wear amber for luck. Other lucky gemstones are Imperial Topaz, yellow diamond and all other yellow to brown crystals and gemstones.

I. The Magician

Number one relates to the tarot card of "The Magician", symbolized by the creator, the inventor and the manifestor. It represents originality and new beginnings. This image shows a woman who is the master of her fate (choices). She has all the tools she needs. She is the vessel, and what is created flows through her, and therefore, her creations reflect her nature.

**2**   Number 2 is ruled by the Moon. The Moon represents needs, especially of an emotional nature, and its sensitivities to emotional and psychic undercurrents. Two reflects an emotional nature that is sentimental and, at times, oversensitive. The quick orbit of the Moon and its phases, can affect twos, making them restless, changeable and moody. This can lead to indecisiveness and a lack of assertiveness. They may be fickle in their desires. They are shy by nature and agreeable, often letting others take the lead. Twos are homebodies. Emotional extremes can lead to emotional suffering and depression, which drains the two's energy and life force. They are very sensitive to their surroundings, and need a peaceful balanced environment. Twos need to learn trust, and to develop positive thinking. The two can experience many ups and downs with finances, until they learn to curb their emotional reactions to money, and make decisions rationally. Partnerships may be helpful in bringing more prosperity to their lives.

Number two and the moon represent the reflected light of the sun. It is the unconscious mind, whereas the number one and the Sun, represent the conscious. Ones and twos can balance and harmonize each other. Twos are also compatible with 4s, but especially with 7s, as 2 and 7 are associated with the intersection points or nodes, in the orbits of the Sun and Moon.

Twos love to travel, and this may make them unsettled, either in their physical location, or in their plans or ideas for the future. Number 2 people are honest, influential, compassionate, romantic, love the arts and are magnetic. They are imaginative and inventive. Twos can live in their heads, and may prefer mental work as opposed to physical, as their physical constitution is not always strong. Despite this, twos ability to rebound from adversity is amazing. Their qualities are more enhanced if born during the Cancer 2-7 Moon period, and seven days thereafter (6/20-7/27).

**Make Plans:** On "2" days (2nd, 11th, 20th, and 29th) especially during the Cancer number 2-7 period (6/20 - 7/27). Secondary are "1", "4" and "7" days.

**Lucky Days:** Sunday, Monday and Friday, especially if a 2, 1, 4 or 7 falls on that day.

**Lucky Colors:** All shades of green, cream and white. Avoid all dark colors, especially black, purple and dark red.

**Lucky Stones:** Wear any shade of jade, especially white and green. Other lucky stones are pearls, moonstones and pale green stones.

The High Priestess tarot card is represented by the number two. Two is the balance of opposites. This card represents intuition, the unconscious mind and the feminine side of the nature. It is the virgin goddess. The bottom of her gown becomes water, flowing out. Water is emotion and the creative imagination. She knows the mysteries of the universe, and has access to all knowledge. The crescent moon is her crown. This card can symbolize a psychic or intuitive person, and all things related to nighttime. It is the undecided and the unknown.

**3** Number three is ruled by the planet Jupiter, which represents wisdom, knowledge, ethics and spirituality. This large planet also symbolizes expansion. Number 3 people care about others, and this makes them attractive and magnetic. This quality is good for business, as well as their gift of witty conversation. All of the above makes them very likable indeed, and others can be swayed by a three's opinions or words, as they can be very outspoken. On the other hand, threes should not get drawn in by what others say, as they can be easily deceived. Threes may tend to be walking encyclopedias, due to their drive for knowledge and understanding, and their ability to retain information. They always land on their feet.

Threes individuals are driven to move to the top of whatever field they endeavor. They are organized and disciplined. They respect rules and guidelines, yet remain very idealistic. They want to control others, and expect them to follow their personal view of how the world should be. They are proud of their active minds, knowledge and accomplishments, and are quite capable and comfortable working for themselves, following their own rules.

Threes can be trusted and relied upon, in positions of authority and disciplined responsibility, such as the government and military. Ultimately, though, threes tend to feel that they know best, and this can create many enemies. They tend have an independent streak, especially if someone else is trying to tie them down, or take away their freedom to do things their own way. Threes are here to learn that commitment and responsibility is freedom, and to birth their own special gift to the world.

**Make Plans:** On "3" days (3rd, 12th, 21st and 30th), especially during the Sagittarius and Pisces number 3 periods (11/21 - 12/20 and 2/19 - 3/20). Secondary are "6" and "9" days.

**Lucky Days:** Thursday, Friday and Tuesday, especially if a 3, 6 or 9 falls on that day.

**Lucky Colors:** Any shade of magenta, violet or purple. Secondary colors are dark maroon, rose, and all shades of blue.

**Lucky Stones:** Wear amethyst. Golden Topaz is also lucky.

The Empress tarot card is a number three, representing  the mom-dad-baby theme, or any grouping of trinities. The number three also has to do with communication. The Empress card represents authority, abundance, fertility, pregnancy and luxury that relate to the expansive qualities of the planet Jupiter, which is linked to the number three and creation. A double three equals a six, related to the planet Venus, its symbol shown on the left (may not be viewable in black and white. See color e-book version). Venus offers the gifts of prosperity and creativity to the three individual. This card can signal pregnancy, the birth of a baby or creative venture, success, happiness and harvest.

**4** Number four is ruled by the Planet Uranus, and Rahu (The North Node of the moon. These nodes are intersection points, on the paths of the Sun and Moon...also called the "head and tail of the dragon".) Four is similar in its energy to the planet Saturn, and thus is related to the number eight. Fours increase eight energy, and like 8s, can be a harbinger of positive or negative karma.

Like their ruler, the planet Uranus, fours rebel or go against the accepted or "normal", and aim for the unconventional or unpredictable. Four individuals like to make their own rules, as they harbor very different views, from others. They can be quarrelsome, insisting on their own viewpoint, or things being their way. In their own rebellion, they unintentionally create the same reaction in others, leading them to rebel against the four, creating much opposition. Fours want to change the rules of everything, from their personal lives. to the world at large. They want to be the authority, and its "my way or no way." Whether they actually do this, or are able to do this, depends on the individual and their circumstances. These Uranus behaviors are also related to Rahu, or the North Node co-rulership. The North Node is all about doing something different, this time around, breaking old patterns and moving forward, into new territories.

Fours have difficulty forming true friendships, but are loyal to the ones they love. Like eights, fours can often feel lonely and depressed. Four's focus is on creating new pathways, and changing the "norm". Some fours follow the traditional rules and standards of society, but will live their life either secretly or openly angry at being "imprisoned" by these regulations. They are seldom focused on money for the sake of money, and therefore may rebel against jobs or careers, that would represent this sole purpose. They can be good at saving money or using it for the causes and people they care about. Fours are much more sensitive than twos, and as a result, tend to bury or ignore feelings, as a method of survival. Emotions are reactionary, and not always easily controlled. The four can feel hurt very deeply, and may therefore choose to stay in their heads, where rational thinking is less threatening. Fours are very practical and persistent, and can be good in business.

As the "4" is a number of fate, the four person should determine whether the number "4" is bringing good karma or misfortune, into their life. If fours prove unlucky, it may be wise to take on the influence of the "1", in your personal numbers.

**Make Plans:** On "4" days, (4th, 13th, 22nd and 31st) especially during the Cancer number 2-7 period and the Leo number 1-4 period (6/21 -8/20).  Secondary are "1", "2" and "7" days.

**Lucky Days:**  Saturday, Sunday and Monday, especially if a 4, 1, 2 or 7 falls on that day.

**Lucky Colors:** Any color a little darker than its pure shade, or lighter, as in pastels; all fluorescent colors, especially bright blue; all gray tones.

**Lucky Stones:**  Wear sapphire. Also Hessonite Garnet is lucky.

The Emperor is the fourth tarot card, representing authority and responsibility. The barren rocky background

IV. The Emperor

suggests rational thought, away from emotional focus. This is an individual who makes the rules, and sees that they are followed. Usually this man is shown wearing armor, which represents a willingness to fight for what he believes in, and for those he protects. He has a loyalty to those he is responsible for, but in its negative aspect of anger, this responsibility becomes controlling, manipulative and overbearing.

**5**   Five's ruler is the planet Mercury. The planet Mercury rules communication, academics and the mind. The element Mercury moves quickly, like water into the path of least resistance, but unlike water, does not stick to anything. If you try to touch mercury, it moves away from your finger. You can't touch it's shape, because it has re-shaped around your finger. When you remove your finger, it rejoins with itself. It has a cold sensation, and can scatter into a bunch of smaller globs, but quickly rejoins back together. It feels slightly heavy in your hand. Number Five people are like Mercury, rebounding from adversity, that does not seem to touch them, and in business, always looking for the quickest or easiest way to make money, or get around things. Hard labor does not appeal to them or their sense of the immediate. Because their minds are so active, they are attuned to new ways of making money, through progressive ideas and inventions. They are risk-takers and investors, prone to buying stocks, or anything that will provide excitement and make a profit quickly.

Decision-making is spontaneous, and fives are adaptable to almost any circumstances. Practicality and everyday life will always suffer, in lieu of these pursuits. Fives will always seem to be making decisions and choosing paths, whether that be in the material or spiritual arenas.

The risks they take can make others nervous, but fives retain the malleable qualities of the element Mercury. Hardship does not affect them, in the same way as it does more sensitive types. Fives don't seem affected by hard times, bouncing away from life's torments as easily as mercury avoids the touch of your fingertip. In no time they are moving on to the next adventure. Fives seem unaffected by life experiences or others attempts to reform them, however, a nervous constitution may cause depression, insomnia or breakdowns in the five. Perhaps they repress their reactions.

Five individuals are easy to get along with, usually having many friends, or others consider them at least a friendly sort. Five can get along well with any other number, but do best with other fives.

Fives excel in the fields of investing, economics, law, advertising, education, promotion, management, entrepreneurism and the arts. Reading or studying the concepts of others who have paved the way, will be very beneficial for a five.

**Make Plans:** On "5" days (5th, 14th and 23rd ), especially during the Gemini and Virgo number 5 Periods (5/21 - 6/20 and 8/21 - 9/20).

**Lucky Days:** Wednesday and Friday, especially if a "5" falls on that day.

**Lucky Colors:** All colors, but the best are light shades, avoiding dark colors. Especially all shades of light gray, white and glittery materials.

**Lucky Stones:** Wear Diamond and platinum. Also all sparkling stones, and silver settings.

The Pope is the fifth tarot card, representing choices and pathways. The number five is one of change or transition.

The Pope gives his blessing, receiving his wisdom from higher sources. His crown shows the three tiers of Father, Son and Spirit. The road symbolizes a crossroads, with different alternatives, one leading to physical desires, the other a spiritual path. The five individual is someone who can give advice or counsel, relating to the five's ability to make decisions, and choose their path, or is seeking higher counsel. There is always movement with the number five. Should one go the conventional road, or take an untried direction?

**6**   Number six is ruled by the planet Venus. Venus has to do with defining what you value in life, financial and material acquisition, and love and beauty in all its aspects. Six people are attracted to beautiful surroundings, the arts, romanticism, and idealism in love. They are very charming, and draw the love of children, partners, co-workers, acquaintances and friends. Love from others can be so important to sixes, that they can get detoured from their own life, in trying to please everyone, and devoting much time and energy into relationships, that may or may not be good for them. This is particularly true of partners. Otherwise, they are very focused and stubborn in doing what they think is best.

In the realm of finances, sixes can be very practical, unless (as mentioned above) they are consumed with pleasing a partner, and allow the other to take charge of the money. If the partner is a spendthrift, this could spell trouble for the six. Because of their love for the finer things in life, the six is willing to spend money on comfort and pleasure. The home is usually filled with artistic pieces, and a place where company is welcome. Beyond a love for the arts, sixes may be gifted themselves in music, poetry, creative writing, painting, dance or creative ideas. Sixes, in general, have abilities in almost anything they put their mind to achieving. They usually attract money later in life.

Usually very gentle and agreeable, a six can become moody or downright angry, if treated with disrespect or abuse from another. They have a strong sense of what is right, and will not back down if they believe in something. A six's lesson in life is to define for themselves, what is truly valuable. This includes their own value, the value of relationships and material values.

**Make Plans:** On "6" days (6th , 15th and 24th) especially during the Taurus and Libra number 6 periods (4/20 - 5/20 and 9/21 - 10/20).  Secondary are "3" and "9" days.

**Lucky Days:** Tuesday, Thursday and Friday, especially if a "6", "3" or "9" falls on those days.

**Lucky Colors:** All shades of blue, rose and pink. Avoid black and dark purple.

**Lucky Stones:** Wear turquoise. Emeralds and Diamonds can also be lucky.

The number Six is represented in "The Lovers" tarot card.  Six is all about relationships, where love is expressed. This card

typically shows Adam and Eve, temptation, sexual desire and its consequences, and all romantic or platonic relationships. The Lovers card has to do with making choices. The "other" comes in and now there is a decision to make. What does one value more? What is the better choice? Where is my desire leading me? It usually means that there is no wrong decision. This card could signal the beginning of a new relationship, or a positive beginning to something.

**7**   The number seven is ruled by the planet Neptune or Ketu – (the South Node of the Moon). Sevens are very attracted to science and nature. This could be mystical or traditional science, and the study of nature, whether that be as a religion, an interest in outdoors or the nature of people.

Ketu can bring sorrow or difficulties, either through malevolence from others, or from the seven's own lack of patience, tenacity, or stubbornness and aloofness toward others. This number seeks aloneness, in order to find their way, and this can cause problems with those who wish for more attention or acquiescence from them. Sevens have the forbearance to endure the sorrows of Ketu, and bounce back from adversity. Developing patience and persistence will turn the hardships into eventual reward, as well as the ability to relieve the sufferings of others. They are prone to support many charitable causes, as the seven can be unconcerned with the accumulation of their own wealth. Their unique minds are capable of excellent ideas for business, so the development of persistence would also serve well here. Sevens are extremely influential, and their unique ideas or mystical depths, often entice others to follow their lead. This can put them in leadership roles, which they may or may not want. Sevens can tend to be outspoken and naive. Just as often, they can be quiet, serene and calming in nature.

Many sevens are here to transcend the mundane, or lower aspects of the nature. They are very original in their views, and adapt well to change, as they have a restless nature like the number two. They get along particularly well, with other sevens and the number two. Seven individuals love travel and other cultures.  Sometimes the acquisition of finances may be difficult for sevens. If this is the case, they will travel in their minds, absorbing information and differing philosophies. They may establish a worldwide or global business with foreign countries. They are drawn to the ocean, and may seek ways to locate close to large bodies of water. The love of water may lead them to own boats, ships or have a love of water sports. Sevens are particularly good writers or artisans. They are likely to consider themselves "spiritual, but not religious", or have their own unique viewpoint, on the teachings of their chosen religion. Neptune gives them the sense of the extraordinary and mysterious. They have great psychic gifts, and many of these come through visions in dreams.

**Make Plans:** On "7" days (7th, 16th and 25th), especially during the Cancer number 2-7 period (6/20 - 7/27). Secondary are "1", "2" and "4" days.

**Lucky Days:** Sunday and Monday, especially if a "7", "1", "2" or "4" falls on these days.

**Lucky Colors:** White. Also fortunate are all shades of green, pastels and yellow. Dark colors are unfortunate.

**Lucky Stones:** Wear moss agate. Also moonstones, cat's eyes and pearls are fortunate.

The Chariot is the seventh tarot card. This represents mastery

over the self and one's nature. This mastery leads to the mystical, and the conquering of any situation. Here, the individual is in a state of meditation, signifying spiritual or celestial influence and guidance. The Chariot is a vehicle, and thereby designed for travel. With self-mastery comes the ability to move forward. Behind the man, in his mer-ka-ba vehicle, is the Sun shining. This card could also relate to issues with a car or travel.

VII. The Chariot

8 Number eight is ruled by Saturn. Saturn teaches us lessons through hard work. It makes us confront our fears. It creates obstacles. It does not deny, but rather delays. It is also the planet of karma, as in, you will reap what you have sown. If you are born under the number 8, you have come into this life to play out the extremes of either positive or negative karma. A life of rewards or payments, decided by justice. Fate seems to control the  eight, as if their lives are crucial to the larger scheme or plan.

For the eight, life can be an uphill battle. They get used to the struggle, and what can be daunting for others, is normal for them. Eights may be hard to read, as their general expression can tend to seem aloof, when in reality, one is seeing their grit and determination. Climbing mountains can be tiresome, and if they are under the hard hand of karma, they may fail, and give up. Eights feel lonely in their struggle, and in their quest to overcome the hardships of Saturn. On the positive side, the challenges give them an understanding and compassion, for those who also suffer. Their fears become their strengths. The drive to overcome adversity, usually leads the eight to climb the ladder of success, or find themselves in higher executive professions, or positions of great responsibility. The price to pay was probably great to get there. A lot of times these positions are in the public eye. An eight, under the influence of reward, may have a fantastical life of luck, money and influence. Whether reward or payment, the challenge of these individuals is to find balance between materialism, and their spiritual or higher nature. As they get older, they may realize that the pursuit of prestige, money, success and the like, has left their lives empty and without meaning. At this stage, a spiritual reference point becomes a necessity.

Eights are very original in their approach, and tend to be extremists in all areas of life. Eights are capable of deep concentration, patience, religious zeal, contemplative analysis, rational thinking, self-control and uncanny business sense.

As the "8" is a number of fate, the eight individual should determine whether the number "8" is bringing good karma or misfortune into their life.

**Make Plans:** On "8" days (8th, 17th and 26th), especially during the Capricorn and Aquarius number 8 periods (12/21 - 2/21). Secondary are "4" days.

**Lucky Days:** Saturday, Sunday and Monday, especially if an "8" or "4" falls on these days.

**Lucky Colors:** Black, navy blue, dark gray and dark purple.

**Lucky Stones:** Wear blue sapphire; also amethyst, darker sapphires, black pearl and black diamond.

(This card was originally the 8th card, but is switched in some

later decks to the 11th position.)[5] Justice is the 8th card, pictured with the Scales of Karma and the Sword of Justice (sword not shown in this image). This card means that justice will be done; the just will be rewarded, and the unjust will pay the price. Eight is the number of power, and all things that represent power, such as money, authority and sex. This card also relates to legal matters, lawyers, contracts, negotiations, striving for an orderly mind, fairness, balance, karma and going to court.

**9**  Number nine is ruled by the planet Mars, a fiery active planet. This number can be subject to danger from fire and accidents. Nines are very bold and adventurous, leaping head first, into the next exciting activity or interest. They may lack patience, and spontaneous or rushed decision-making or

---

[5] The Tarot: History, Symbolism and Divination, by Robert Place

temperament, can cause problems in life. Others may resent their hurried approach. Hurrying makes them more susceptible to injury, from the aforementioned dangers, and many failures can be a result, of avoiding contemplation before action.

Nines are capable of being practical and organized. Nine's willful intensity, can often be interpreted as anger by others. This is not always the case, although, anger can become an issue. Mars nines have a fighting spirit. In the less evolved, this may come out as a violent, war-like nature. In the more self-aware, nines can be a fighter, for what they see as right, such as an activist, or standing up for the needs of loved ones and themselves. Childhood may be difficult, as they have a lack of control, over what happens to them. There may be many issues from family, that plague the adult nine throughout their life. They need to make peace with the past. Nines usually succeed, by their willpower and drive, to get what they want. They are not so good in subordinate positions, and do better calling the shots. This could apply to home life or career. If they are not in charge, they are not interested, or their heart will not be in it. Nine is a fortunate number, as long as the lower nature is overcome, and the fiery temperament controlled. When the number 9 is repetitive in the native's life, it is a doubling of the nine. This can increase the likelihood of the negative attributes of this number, leading to an increase in conflict, quarrels, accidents and opposition.

Mars, being the planet of war, can lead these people to an attraction for the military, martial arts, government, or to become leaders of a cause. There is also an attraction to find a soulmate or partner, and sometimes this may prove to be a difficult task.  The nine craves love (Venus), and (Mars) will do whatever it takes to find it. Nines can have a strong body or constitution, and may be good at sports or physical activity.

**Make Plans:** On "9" days (9th, 18th and 27th), especially during the Aries and Scorpio number 9 periods (3/21 - 4/19 and 10/21 - 11/20).  Secondary are "3" and "6" days.

**Lucky Days:** Tuesday, Thursday and Friday, especially if a "9", "3" or "6" falls on that day.

**Lucky Colors:**   All tones of crimson, red, rose and pink, relating to the red planet Mars.

**Lucky Stones:** Wear ruby, garnet, coral and bloodstone.

The Hermit is the ninth tarot card. Nine represents the ending of cycles (as nine added to itself equals nine), or the

repeating of cycles (as nine added to any other number will repeat that number). The Hermit is here to lead. The fire on his candle lights the way. The six-pointed star of Venus, symbolizing love and peace and the search for self-love, is also the Seal of Solomon, which means protection. It represents attributes, for which a nine should be striving. This is accomplished through the ways of the Hermit: Finding alone time, away from others, for contemplation, and learning control of the temperament. This card also means to act on faith. One is not alone, as spirit guides and angels are assisting the individual. One is traveling the correct path, although it may not feel as if this is the case.

# Natural Harmonies

**1**   harmonizes with 1, 4, 2, 7.

-avoid 4 if this number seems to represent karmic debt for the 1 individual.

**2**   harmonizes with 2, 7, 1, 4.

- avoid 8 (2 may attract 8s because 2 + 2 + 2 + 2 = 8. *Four* of this number increases the 8 energy, and brings suffering to the 2 ).

-can have luck with 6, because 2 + 2 + 2 = 6. *Three* of this number supports the six (although six is still not considered in the same harmonious series as the 2).

**3**   harmonizes with 3, 6, 9.

**4**   harmonizes with 4, 1, 2, 7.

- avoid doubling the 4(as it makes an 8), and avoid 8, if it represents karmic debt for the individual.

- avoid 9.

**5**   harmonizes best with 5; in a general sense with all numbers.

**6**   harmonizes with 6, 3, 9.

-has luck with 2, because *three* twos equal six, and support the six (2 + 2 + 2 = 6), and two threes equal six (although two is still not considered in the same harmonious series as the 6).

**7**   harmonizes with 7, 2, 1, 4.

- avoid 8.

**8**   harmonizes with 8, 4.

- avoid 7 and 9.

- avoid 4 and 8 if they represent karmic debt for the individual.

**9**   harmonizes with 9, 3, 6.

- avoid 4 and 8.

The "3", "6" and "9" flow together, because any of these numbers, added together, will equal one of their own series. 3 + 6 = 9; 3 + 3 = 6; 6 + 6 = 12/3; 9 + 3 = 12/3; 9 + 9 = 18/9; 9 + 6 = 15/6. The 6 is divided equally by two "3s". The "9" is divided equally by three "3s".

The "1", "2", "4" and "7" are in harmony, through their connections to the Sun and Moon. One and two are connected, because the "2" can be equally divided by "1". Four can be equally divided by two, and "1" and "2" are ruled by the Sun and Moon respectively. The numbers "4" and "7" vibrate with Uranus and Neptune, in western astrology, and with the North and South Nodes of the Moon, in ancient astrology (which are crossover points on the paths of the Sun and Moon). Seven is not equally dividable, and stands by itself, having "loner" or unique characteristics.

The number "5" is ruled by Mercury, and compatible with other "5s". In a secondary sense, it gets along with all numbers, because of the fluidity and adaptability of its Mercury nature. Five is also not equally divisible, so it is unique to itself.

The "4" and "8" are connected, as the "8" can be divided equally by the "4". These two are therefore drawn to each other, but can bring much karma and difficulty, as their ruling planets, Saturn and Uranus, do not get on well together. Otherwise eights should be with eights, or avoided altogether.

# What's Your Real Birthstone?

You will notice, that your Day Number gemstones, may be different from what you have been told is your "birthstone". It is common knowledge that if you are born in July, your traditional birthstone is a ruby. These  commercialized birth stones may have been created, by jewelers based on what was easy to create in jewelry, or in ready supply. It is not really known whether these "birth stones" actually have a connection to you, your day of birth or your birth month.

The ancient sciences of Chaldean and Hindu Numerology and Astrology studied the patterns of numbers, and their connection to the heavenly bodies. These number patterns related to specific planets, timing, gemstones, human characteristics and patterns of fate. Gemstones reflect heavenly light. Our bodies are made up of the same minerals as gemstones and crystals. Each of our cells has a positive or negative magnetic charge, consisting of protons and electrons. Our system is electrical and magnetic. Everything around us has a magnetic charge.  When we wear gems, they react with light, altering the electromagnetic field of the body, and thereby creating an electrochemical balance in the body. These stones are charged through exposure to the Sun, Moon, stars and planetary bodies within our solar system, attuning to certain fields of magnetic energy, through their color spectrum, and compositional makeup or structure.  In turn, they are connected to specific planets (Sun and Moon included as "planets" here) which individually rule times of the year, on our calendar, or months. These gemstones also relate to the days of the month, as the planets rule certain number vibrations.

What does all this mean? Your *day* of birth and *month* of birth are ruled, by particular stones of a certain color vibration. These stones help to alter detrimental energy, or increase your good luck, by wearing and carrying them with you.

## Gemstones That Rule the Day of Birth

### Born on the 1st, 10th, 19th or 28th of any month
Yellow Topaz, Amber, Yellow Diamond. Also Ruby.

### Born on the 2nd, 11th, 20th or 29th
Pearl, Moonstone, pale green stones and Green Jade. Also Clear Quartz and Green or White Agate.

### Born on the 3rd, 12th, 21st, 30th
Amethyst. Also Yellow Sapphire and Yellow Topaz.

### Born on the 4th, 13th, 22nd, 31st
Blue Sapphire. Also Hessonite (garnet).

### Born on the 5th, 14th, 23rd
Diamond, glittery stones, set in Platinum, Silver. Also, Emerald.

### Born on the 6th, 15th, 24th
Turquoise and Emeralds. Also, White Diamond, White Sapphire, White Zircon, White Tourmaline.

### Born on the 7th, 16th, 25th
Moonstone, Pearl, Moss Agate, Cat's Eye (non-synthetic), set in White Gold.

### Born on the 8th, 17th, 26th
Amethyst, Dark Sapphires, Black Pearl, Black Diamond.

### Born on the 9th, 18th, 27th
Ruby, Garnet, Bloodstone (if not worn next to skin). White or Red Coral, Carnelian and Jasper.

## Gemstones That Rule the Month

(In a more general sense, and for secondary use)

**January** - Moonstones, Pearls, Amethyst

**February** - Sapphires, Pink Topaz, Moonstone

**March** - Agate, Sapphire, Amethyst, Emerald

**April** - Rubies, Garnets, Bloodstone

**May** - Emerald, Turquoise, Lapis Lazuli

**June** - White or Red Carnelian, Sapphire, Diamond, Glittery gems

**July** - Pearl, Diamond, Opal, Cat's Eyes, Clear Quartz, Moonstone

**August** - Imperial and White Topaz, Amber, Ruby

**September** - Emerald, Diamond, Pearl

**October** - Opal, Pearl

**November** - Turquoise, Ruby, all red stones

**December** - Amethyst, Sapphire

# Compound Numbers & Their Meanings

The compound numbers 10-52 are the higher vibrations of the single numbers, and also have specific meanings of their own. Compound numbers show the workings of fate, or outside forces that control our destiny, and act on us. This influence is not always apparent or expected. These compound numbers are prognosticators of future events.

**10** The number ten is symbolized as the "Wheel of Fortune". It is a number of intentions, or personal agendas. Depending on one's honor, or lack thereof, this number denotes a rise to fame and fortune, but just as easily a fall. It bestows self-confidence and having faith. Ten deals with all issues of faith; including others trust in you and trusting yourself. It is considered a fortunate number, because one's plans will usually work out.

The tenth card, in the tarot deck, is the "Wheel of Fortune".

This card deals with the law of karma and grace. One is learning and growing spiritually, through one's experiences. It represents the unknown future, coming up suddenly over the horizon. We cannot see it, until it is upon us. What was meant to happen, will happen. Ten is a new beginning; a smarter beginning, because one has been around the wheel once already. This image contains the symbols for Jupiter and Saturn, representing luck and hard lessons, respectively. The wheel always creates new beginnings, and brings around old endings that were not resolved. One's fortune is based on one's intentions; you will reap what you sow, or have sown.

X. Wheel of Fortune

**11**   The eleven is symbolized by a lion's mouth being covered, or  closing the mouth of a lion, with bare hands; also a clenched hand or fist, as if in frustration or holding back. It represents being up against great difficulties, threats that you are unaware of, underhanded betrayals, trouble, suffering, opposition and endangerment from others. The person it represents may get into trouble from speaking their mind, or opening their mouth in certain circumstances. In some cases, the person has learned from this number, when it is best to remain silent, or refrain from acting out of anger or cruelty.

In modern decks, the "Strength" card is listed as number

eight, but was originally the eleventh card. Traditionally, it contains the imagery of the lion's mouth, being closed by a woman. This shows control of the ego and the desires of the lower self. In older decks, a man is beating the lion. The halo above her head, symbolizes wisdom and mastery gained through overcoming the ego, as love conquers all. This card can also be perceived as closing the mouth of our negative thoughts and words.

**12**   The twelve is symbolized by sacrifice, and can literally mean becoming *a sacrifice or a victim,* in every sense. This number predicts that you  may be subject to, or sacrificed for the plotting and self-interests of others, or something you value is sacrificed. It is a number of suffering, and having issues with long term mental worry, anxiety and stress.

A traditional meaning, for the twelfth tarot card of "The Hanged Man", is sacrifice, suffering, grief or loss. If one views

this hanging man, as an unmoving pendulum, of sorts, the meaning can also represent being stuck in a limbo. Sacrifice can bring things to a halt, or prevent further progress. There is an aura of light around his head, signifying illumination and wisdom, gained through getting a different view of life, during this pause or stasis. The root number three suggests communication from Spirit, when one stands still to listen. Twelve also deals with the future. What has been prophesied will come to pass.

**13**   This is a fortunate number, represented by the symbolism of the ultimate powers of death and renewal, and those with this number can have power and dominance over others. The thirteen is a number of drastic change and death, so that something new can be born in its place. It signifies transformation. This includes changes in locations, agendas, relationships, goals and plans. These disruptions, dissolutions and endings are usually permanent, and for the better.

The key to harnessing the good energy of this number, is to flow with change, surrender, move forward and embrace the transformations. In this, is great personal power to be found, or rather recognized. Death has its own timing. To deliberately affect drastic change or death, leads to the destruction of the self, whether metaphorically or literally, and loss of power or influence. This number warns of unanticipated and unforeseen circumstances, for the future.

In ancient tarot decks, a skeleton is shown with a sickle or  scythe. In the Rider Waite deck, the skeleton is riding a white horse, trampling anyone who gets in the way. This includes the Pope, whose authority and power is of the manmade world, and even he cannot escape the powers of life, death and rebirth. The ego creates a false sense of power and security, believing that we are invincible. Nothing stands in the way of death, and therefore, the challenge is to succumb and wait to be reborn. In this particular image, we see "Death" ruling over our universe. Death defines our world, and keeps us stuck in the reincarnation cycle. Thirteen also symbolizes the death of the ego-self. Four, which is the root number, suggests transformation is needed, to create stability, security and benefit, for the one transformed. Death signifies change that has been desired, and is permanent.

**14**   The number 14 reduces to a "5". Five is a fortunate number, and represents change. Things are stirred up with this number, as mixtures and combinations come together to make a greater creation. This includes combining groups of people or things, to attain certain results. Fourteen warns of natural catastrophes, in combinations of air, fire and water, such as tornadoes, hurricanes, blizzards, forest fires and thunderstorms. These dangers can also be related to fire, water and air conditions in the physical body and organs. The fourteen also warns of trusting others to make decisions, plans or take action on your behalf. Since the five represents change, any alterations in business, career or money planning should go well, however, the wrong combination of people or circumstances can ruin a venture. This number can access the

positive qualities of the root number five, if one uses conservative judgment, and acts with discernment, wisdom, and above all, constraint and patience. Fourteen individuals may have a talent for communication, through writing or speaking.

"Temperance" tames the "tempests" warned of in the fourteen. This tarot card shows two angels combining liquids, to achieve the right combination. This creates balanced manifestations, that are in harmony with Spirit. The rainbow spiral signifies being in agreement with Source, and can represent the light spectrum, as well as the chakras. Things are in a state of change, with the root number five. Balance must be maintained.

**15**   This enigmatic number represents attractions, and the allure of the material side of life. It can be very influential and fortunate, when combined with harmonious or supported numbers. The person it represents can have a passionate and powerful make-up. They have a sensual nature, are very appealing or desirable, may be talented in music, art or drama and make excellent speakers. It is a lucky number, for obtaining financial assistance, support and gifts.

When the numbers "4" and "8" are associated with fifteen, the darker side of this number manifests. It represents motivations and temptations, that can lead a person to do whatever it takes to get what they want, without a second thought. The individual is focused completely on self, and gaining what they desire. They will go to any lengths, or they themselves can become involved, with groups or practices with ill or evil intent.

Fifteen is a number to be careful with, because it can also draw in elements of a darker nature, associated with black magic, dark entities, an addictive partner and the like. This number can represent, in its extremes of dark expression, being possessed, entity attachments, addictions and all other consequences of messing with, or being involved in dark side energy. This includes bad luck. Fifteen can be very fortunate and dynamic, if fours and eights are not combined with this number. If they are avoided, one can work with the benefits of this number, and avoid the warnings.

"The Devil" tarot card is an ominous looking image. Adam and Eve are shown here, chained to a demon entity. The background is growing dark, alluding to ignorance of the

XV. The Devil

truth, and darkness of the soul. The demon symbol could relate to any addiction, misery, a person or dark entity, that has chained the individual. Keep in mind, the person represented could also be the demon in this image, controlling others through manipulation, temptation and force. On its positive side, this card relates to the enjoyment of the material world, pleasure and gain.

**16** Sixteen is called the "Shattered Citadel", and its symbolism is a crowned tower, being hit by lightning, with people falling from it. These images allude to drastic change and changes in power. This number warns of one's plans being destroyed, quite suddenly and unexpectedly, especially if the individual is caught up in the ego and false power. Its root number seven represents a spiritual lesson and transition. It predicts deadly or dangerous accidents. These could include actual falls, as seen in the tarot card, or blows to the head. It can also represent a quite sudden failure or loss of a venture. Although sixteen can be fortunate for a time, it is a warning sign for the future, and one should make back-up plans, to avoid the destructive possibilities of this number.

"The Tower" card represents quick and sudden forced changes, caused by the higher self or outside forces, based on resistance to change from the individual. This is usually a destructive force, that tears down what has been built. This image symbolizes, that a change in power is needed. The higher self destroys, what the ego has built. This card could symbolize abrupt endings, in the individual's life, such as plans, businesses, partnerships and the like. It may represent problems with the home, land, electrical disturbances and

psychic energies. The encroaching dark storm here, suggests a turning away from the higher nature. Being too caught up in the physical realm, and its false sense of power, that was entered into with the Devil card. The higher nature shakes you out of this prison, and frees the soul. The blackening sky represents ignorance and lack of spiritual truth, which make the change here feel sudden and destructive. This is a quick  change, unlike the Death card transition. Lightning can allude, to problems with anything electrical, or an actual thunderstorm.

**17**   Seventeen is called the "Star of the Magi", and is represented by the eight-pointed "star" as it appears to us in the sky. This is Venus, the planet of love, peace and true inner or spiritual beauty. This is a sacred number, representing the

higher powers of divinity and real love. This person has overcome adversity, and developed themselves spiritually in a past life, or in this life. They have attained a certain level of karmic reward, overcoming many of the struggles and hardships of life or career. It is the "Immortality Number", and the name of the person it represents will live on after their departure or death. It is a lucky number if it is not combined with the single numbers, four or eight.

   "The Star" card represents the hope, that comes after the

destruction, of the Tower. The number "17" reduces to an "8", relating to power, and all things that represent power, in this world, such as money, sex and authority. Here, however, is an enlightened version of the "8", suggesting the overcoming of the ego, in the 16th card, leading to a sense of peace and wisdom. The woman dips into still waters of Spirit, and is nourished. The water represents abundance, and the green grass could allude to money. Because this is an eight, this card could suggest having enough money, to start putting into savings. It is also a card that represents healing. The star in the background represents Venus, as well as other galaxies, worlds and dimensions.

**18**    Eighteen is symbolized as a moon emanating the reflected light of the sun, with drops of blood, falling into the opened mouths of a wolf and dog. A crayfish is coming out of the water below them. Eighteen can be fortunate, because it is a nine, but it is a perplexing number. The animals in this imagery, represent our animal or ego tendencies, striving to overpower our divine nature. This individual can become lost in materialism, losing track of the true spiritual self. This is the battle between the spiritual nature, and the lower self. This number can bring about the negative qualities of the nine, attracting betrayal, deceit and danger from natural or man-made sources, involving water and fire, such as storms, house fires, flooding, and explosions. Eighteen can bring in conflict, warfare, family discord, uprisings, rebellions and the like, or a profiting from these.

Although it is often a lucky number, its influence is dual. Because the moon represents things that are hidden, there are strong warnings with the eighteen, of betrayal and duplicity from others, and unexpected dangers. To avoid the above, utilize the advice given for the number nine, and its rules.

The 18th tarot card is "The Moon". Traditionally a dog and wolf, are pictured with a crayfish. Sometimes this is a crab,

relating to the sign Cancer, which is ruled by the Moon. In older decks, the dog and wolf are catching drops of blood in their mouths. The droplets could be related to dew, which forms at night. Dew is represents, in alchemy, the Divine, and is often purported to drop from heaven. In ancient writings, it was believed to be produced by the plant life, giving up their essence into the air. As drops of blood, this would signify the life force, and again relate to alchemy. (The droplets are said to be Yahs, the name of the Egyptian Moon god.) This card symbolizes the light of the moon, when things are hidden, or not out in the light of day. It could represent deceit, hidden agendas, psychic abilities, phases of the moon, eclipses or the unknown.

**19** Nineteen is called the "Prince of Heaven", and "The Sun".

This is a benign number, assuring admiration from others, joy, recognition, success and happiness. It may bring children into your life. Overall, this is an extremely lucky number.

The nineteenth card is called "The Sun". It is a happy card, suggesting success, joy and celebration. Things that were hidden, are clear. In this image, we see a small child, relating to the birth of a child, or the return of the "sun god". This could also be related, to the birth of Jesus, the Son of God, who is known as the "Prince of Heaven". The white horse symbolizes power, the conquering of the ego, and the return to truth. The lack of clothing is the ridding of the ego self, and being re-born in Spirit.

**20**  Twenty is called the "Awakening", and "Judgement". It is a vision of an angel sounding a trumpet, and a man, woman and child rising from their tombs, with arms lifted up in supplication. Individuals with this number can have extremely painful childhoods. To find  solace, they must learn to cope with the residual emotional damage, by growing spiritually. One may feel a calling, toward a specific or particular life purpose or obligation. The individual has incarnated, to complete their mission. They have chosen painful circumstances, to elicit a "wake up call" or response, toward developing the higher nature. Success with this number is determined by spiritual or soul progress, not material value. Therefore, accomplishment in a worldly sense, may or may not have been in the individual's plan, when incarnating.

Because of the imagery of people rising from the grave, individuals with this number can be obsessed with death, be responsible for the death of others, or be drawn to mediumship or anything to do with death, dying and the other side. When looking for a favorable day in the future, this number may bring setbacks, obstacles and delays, until one has learned to look to their higher nature, for guidance.

XX. Judgement

The 20th tarot card is "Judgement". This card is a wake up call, with Archangel Gabriel, announcing the news of the body's return to Spirit. It is a calling, to drop off the physical body and the veil of illusions, and connect with the true spiritual nature. This card also refers to the receiving of some sort of message, whether directly, through angels, Spirit, ideas or inspiration. Because it is a double ten, it represents new beginnings at a faster rate. Everything is at a higher vibration, and therefore sped up. This is a card of messages, heralding something good. It is the Age of Aquarius.

**21**   Twenty-one is called "The Universe" or "The Crown of the Magi". It represents a lengthy process, of overcoming the world, through tests and trials that require fortitude. Eventually, the individual will triumph over these challenges. It is a number of progress and overall success, achieving prestige, recognition and distinction. It is considered a fortunate number of success.

The triumph over "The World" and its karma is represented by this trump ("triumph") tarot card, number twenty-one. This relates to success in the world, or liberation from the ego's world of illusions. This is the exiting from the cycle of karma and reincarnation. It can represent a portal into other dimensions, worlds or the angelic realms. It can mean worldly gain, freedom, world travel, and access to other worlds. Wisdom has been achieved, and the learning is complete.

**22** Twenty-two is pictured as a well-intentioned, yet vulnerable man. He is oblivious, to a vicious tiger attacking him, because he is dazed and lost in his own daydreaming. He can be fooled by others, or lured into danger, remaining unaware of another's foolishness, until it is too late. He carries a symbolic satchel over his shoulder, filled with his missteps, misplaced trust, and blunders. Twenty-two is a warning number. These individuals are good people, but may live in a fantasy world of naivety and pipe dreams. It represents an honorable person who lives in a state of enjoyment, based on false beliefs or hopes; a state of illusory happiness, when one may actually be surrounded by fools. This person can also make bad decisions, due to the influence of others. It therefore

XXII. The Fool

carries the warning of illusions, deceptions and deluding oneself.

"The Fool" card is the 22nd tarot card, sometimes pictured as zero. It represents complete freedom from the world. One has exited through the portal of the "World" card, and gained truth, mastery and safety. The zero is the escape from all numbers, beginnings and endings. If one's lessons are not learned, and attachments released, however, the individual is sent back to the beginning, to reincarnate again. We see this here, as the child is about to step in to the hole. For the enlightened, this is a card of trust and faith. To the outside world, and those who conform to worldly agendas, and have not yet seen the wisdom of truth, one can appear as a fool, when acting outside the norm. The fool has the King's ear. He has nothing to lose. He knows something we don't. On the other hand, this card can represent someone who blindly trusts in others, and does not pay attention. This card can mean taking risks, doing things you haven't done before, and new beginnings. The inverted rainbow, here (with red on the inside) signifies a being who has left the world and entered Heaven.

> *Our modern tarot decks were redesigned with 22 Trump Cards or Major Arcana. It is not known how many trumps were in the original tarot decks, as there were no specimens found fully intact. One of these prototype decks had over forty trumps[6], leading us to surmise that the original decks had 52 trumps, relating to all 52 Chaldean numbers, in accordance with the creation of the Chaldean week (there are 52 weeks in a year).*

**23**   Twenty-three is a highly fortunate number, called the "Royal Star of the Lion." It ensures success, assistance and support from higher-ups, or those in positions to help the individual. It also implies the individual is protected in some way. Twenty-three guarantees success in one's endeavors.

**24**   This number is very fortunate. It attracts alliances, with those in high positions to help the individual achieve their goals. There is an allure, that attracts love ties and amorous relationships, that can also be beneficial. This is a number of success.

**25**   Twenty-five is a number symbolizing strength, obtained by enduring hardships of the past. The experience of conflict has taught the individual to scrutinize their surroundings and

---

[6] The Tarot: History, Symbolism and Divination by Robert Place

other people, and they benefit from this insight. This is a very auspicious number.

**26**  Twenty-six carries a very serious warning of destruction or loss, caused by association with others; gambling, taking risks, misinformation, partnerships, mergers and alliances. It is a warning number for future plans.

**27**  Twenty-seven is very fortunate, and is symbolized by "The Scepter", relating to the "wands" or "staffs" in tarot. The scepter and wand indicate authority and creativity. This number signifies being in charge, having responsibility, and power and influence over others. The ideas of the creative intelligence will find fertile ground, and produce a harvest. A good number if one follows their own ideas and plans.

**28**  Individuals with this number show great potential, promise and possibility for success. Twenty-eight carries with it many inconsistencies, and the probability of having to constantly start over with projects, goals and life. Because of these reversals, these individuals should attentively plan and save for the future. It foretells of danger and loss in lawsuits or the law, loss through placing confidence or trust  in others, and rivalry and competition in business. Not a lucky number when connected to future plans.

**29**  Twenty-nine carries with it many serious warnings. Love relationships can be ill-fated, filled with heartache, betrayals and dishonesty. This number indicates false friends, as well as unforeseen hardships and disasters. It is a warning number for future plans.

**30**   Thirty can be one of the most powerful numbers, but it is up to the choice or will of the person it represents. This person has highly developed mental faculties, and lives in their mind. It is up to them to decide what they value, and what is important to them in life. Often, they are not interested in, or satisfied with worldly or materialistic goals. They possess the ability to determine what their lot in life will be. Therefore, the auspiciousness of this number is entirely up to their interpretation and desires.

**31**   Thirty-one is also a highly cognitive number. This individual is not only isolated in their mind, but from others, as well. It is a lonely number, and not fortunate for matters of the world or material gain, because the individual is cut-off from the world around him in some way.

*After 31, we have surpassed possible numbers related to the Day Number. Beyond this point are special lessons and some repetitions of earlier numbers. Number 32 symbolizes "The Paths of Wisdom". This signals the next set of numbers, representing opportunities to overcome the challenges of earlier numbers, and particular karma (as 32-through 52 will only be found connected to the name or Hidden Number). These are played out in this life, balancing out old karma, or creating new.*

**32**   Thirty-two is called "The Paths of Wisdom", and is a fortunate number, with the magical power of its root number "five". Its karma is similar to "14" and "23", but this number has to do with groups of people, communities, countries or society as a whole. People with this number are influenced by the willfulness of others, and may ruin set plans or goals, by following other's ignorance or incompetence. These individuals have the *wisdom of this number,* which brings good fortune, so they should follow their own advice, and rely on their own intelligence and understanding, of all matters and plans for the future.

**33**   Has the same karma as 24.

**34**   Has the same karma as 25.

**35**   Has the same karma as 26.

**36**   Thirty-six has the same karma as "27". It is also wholeness, as it is the number of the original 36 constellations, mapped by the Chaldeans, as taught to the Egyptians. (It relates to the 36 decans in modern astrology.) Thirty-six suggests that the individual has come into this incarnation, to master the traits and challenges connected to all additional 36 constellation signs. It also relates to the astrological wheel of 360 degrees, coming full circle, and symbolically conquering the ego construct. This could, in some cases, represent the individual is here for their final lifetime.

**37**   Thirty-seven has definitive characteristics all its own. It is a partnership number, bringing healthy happy relationships, friendships, love and positive associations of all kinds, including business and personal. It is a fortunate number.

**38**   Has the same karma as 29.

**39**   Has the same karma as 30.

**40**   Has the same karma as 31.

**41**   Has the same karma as 32.

**42**   Has the same karma as 24.

**43**   Forty-three is not a fortunate number. It is symbolized by the energy of power plays, stirring up opposition, revolutions, conflicts, defeats and failures.

**44**   Has the same karma as 26.

**45**   Has the same karma as 27.

**46**   Has the same karma as 37.

**47**   Has the same karma as 29.

**48**  Has the same karma as 30. Forty-eight is the total number of zodiac constellations - the 12 as we know today (narrowed down by the Greeks), and the three nearby, that correspond to each of these twelve. This is a number of totality and completion on this earth plane.

**49**  Has the same karma as 31.

**50**  Has the same karma as 32.

**51**  Fifty-one has the definitive characteristics of a warrior and fighter. It is a fortunate number for those in positions of leadership, those in the military, or any profession or cause one has to fight for, bringing swift support, fast promotion and progress, for all ventures. Because of its war-like nature, this number warns of enemies, threats to one's well-being and possibilities of assassination or decimation of character.

**52**  Has the same karma as 43.

*All numbers, after 52, share the energy of the number they equal, such as 85 = 13, and so on.*

For more clarity, here is a break down of which numbers are considered either fortunate or unlucky:

**Fortunate:**  10, 19, 21, 23, 24, 25, 27, 30, 32, 33, 34, and so on.

**Unfortunate:**  11, 12, 22, 26, 28, 29, 31, 35, and so on.

**Dual in Nature:**  13, 14, 15, 16, 17, 18, 20

(Explained in more detail in Chapter Six.)

# CHAPTER THREE

# The Name Numbers

W hat's in a name? Everything. Each letter of our alphabet has a number value assigned to it, and therefore shares a vibrational frequency with that number. According to Chaldean Numerology, aspects of your personality and fate reside in these seemingly meaningless identifiers. Finding your Name Numbers is simply adding together the numbers assigned to each letter in your name. Your name numbers are important, because *they are the only numbers that can be changed,* thereby allowing you to modify the other numbers, and your course of destiny.

*This form of numerology is just one, of many systems,*
*with numbers assigned to letters. Each of these methods*
*are for differing purposes, and should be contained*
*within its own rules. Two well-known systems include*
*Gematria and Pythagorean.*

Why would you want to change your name? Many people change their names, because of marriage, dislike of a given name, using a nickname, anonymity in business, etc. Using Chaldean Numerology to create a lucky name, can bring success, and free you from many undesirable experiences or failures. Unfortunate circumstances could be drawn to you, should you choose to continue to live under the influence of an unlucky name.

Fortunate name numbers help create a lucky Hidden Number, and support the Day Number. I will guide you through the name-changing process in Chapter Six, "Change Your Numbers; Change Your Luck".

The numbers assigned to letters are as follows:

## The Chaldean Alphabet

| 1 | 2 | 3 | 4 | 5 | 6 | 7 | 8 |
|---|---|---|---|---|---|---|---|
| A | B | C | D | E | U | O | F |
| I | K | G | M | H | V | Z | P |
| J | R | L | T | N | W |   |   |
| Q |   | S |   | X |   |   |   |
| Y |   |   |   |   |   |   |   |

*Note: There is not a letter value for 9. Nine is considered the
number  related to the name of God, who represents all of
totality, and is outside the influence of fate. God is completion
and oneness. Any number added to nine, repeats itself
(needing to go back and repeat the karma or learn the lesson
again). Therefore nine is omitted from this alphabet system.*

Since you were given your name at birth, *the name
numbers represent present karma being created in this lifetime.* This
means, as your name is spoken and used, karma is created,
based on the numbers found in your name. Just as you can
modify karma from previous lifetimes, by your present choices
and actions in this life, so too does the use of your name help
modify or negate old karma, and create present and future
karma. Your name numbers, then, help attract what happens
to you in the future, whether good or bad.

Assigning the Chaldean numbers to letters in a name is
simple:

| M | a | r | y | | J | o | n | e | s |
|---|---|---|---|---|---|---|---|---|---|
| 4 | 1 | 2 | 1 | | 1 | 7 | 5 | 5 | 3 |

*The name numbers assist in creating the Hidden Number,
which also predicts fate or upcoming circumstances in life. The
"name numbers" consist of the Individual Name Number (INN)
and the Total Name Number (TNN).*

## The Individual Name Number (INN)

Most of us use more than one name. We usually have a first,
middle and last name. The Individual Name Number, or INN,
is found by adding up the letters in each of your names,

separately.

When adding up the letters of your name, you want to use *the name you are most known by*, which may not necessarily be the name you were given at birth. The name you are most often called by, might be a nickname. If you were born with the name Richard Jones, but are always called "Rick", you would calculate for "Rick Jones". Rick Jones would have two INNs. Madonna would have a single INN, but if she used her last name privately, she would have a first INN and a last INN. Another person with a single INN or two INNs would be the singer Beyonce. Even though her last name is Knowles, the use of her last name has diminished, and she is commonly known as "Beyonce". In the news, a headline would read, "Beyonce performing at Super Bowl half time!" There would be no need to use her last name, as it might seem unusual to see "Beyonce Knowles, performing at Super Bowl half time!" Jennifer Lopez would have two INNs, "Jennifer", and "Lopez". Being known sometimes as "J. Lo", would also give her two INNs, the "J" and "Lo" would be added separately. Both of these names would have an influence on her life.

Example 1: John Smith - Two INN's - "John" and "Smith"

Example 2: John Smith Jr. - Three INN's - "John", "Smith" and the title "Jr."

Example 3: A person is always known publicly, using initials in his name, such as "Michael W. Smith". The "W" would be a separate INN, as well as "Michael" and "Smith". He would have 3 INN's in this name, and therefore three name number totals.

More examples: If you are born with the name "Jonathan Smith", but are known as "Jon Smith", you would calculate the INNs for "Jon Smith". Any add-ons or titles are added separately as well. "Prince Harry" would add the letters for "Prince" and "Harry" separately. *Any titles that are temporary, or for a short duration of time would not be used.*

## How to Calculate the INN

Assign the number value from the Chaldean Alphabet to each letter of the name, and add them together.   Here are the two INNs of my name added separately:

    1   5   4   1   2   1   5
    A   n   m   a   r   i   e
    1 + 5 + 4 + 1 + 2 + 1 + 5 = 19
    The INN for "Anmarie" is **19**.


    6   2   5   2
    U   b   e   r
    6 + 2 + 5 + 2 = 15
    The INN for "Uber" is **15**.


Note:  In this example, my name Anmarie has an INN of "19". This compound number would influence my life. Nineteen has a very fortunate meaning, so this is an INN I would want to keep, as long as it harmonizes with my other destiny numbers correctly, to produce more fortunate numbers.  The same would go for my last name INN of "15". Both of these INNs can be reduced to their root numbers of "1" and "6", respectively, and written as "19/1" and "15/6".

# The Total Name Number (TNN)

Adding together the separate totals of each INN root number will give you the Total Name Number or TNN. Remember, *the TNN needs to be in harmony with your Day Number, in order to avoid the effects of any other unlucky numbers, and to have balance in your life and affairs.* This is very important. If these two numbers are not in accord, your life will not flow, and be chaotic with many obstacles to contend with in your career and personal endeavors. You could also, as mentioned, suffer the effects of any unfortunate numbers that have no harmonious support (see "Unsupported Numbers" in Chapter Six under "Rules for Numbers"). I will show options on how to harmonize the TNN and Day Number in Chapter Six.

## How to Calculate the TNN

To find the Total Name Number (TNN), add together *the single or root number* INNs:

Example 1:  Anmarie = **19**   $(1 + 9 = 10; 1 + 0) = $ **1**

The single  INN number for Anmarie is **1**.

Uber = 15   $(1 + 5) = $ **6**

The single INN number for Uber is **6**.

To arrive at our TNN for Anmarie Uber, you would add the reduced single numbers of each name, $1 + 6 = 7$. *The TNN for Anmarie Uber is 7.* (There is no compound number for her TNN, because the 1 added to the 6 did not produce a compound number.)

Example 2:  George Clooney

George = **25/7**

Clooney = **31/4**

7 + 4 = **11**

The TNN for George Clooney is the compound number 11, which reduces to 2, (as 1 + 1 = 2).

# CHAPTER FOUR

# The Hidden Number: Unforeseen Pitfalls & Blessings

When the Day and Total Name Number (TNN) are added together, they reveal another number that can have power over your life, if you remain unaware of its existence. This number is called the "Hidden Number". The Hidden Number is an important personal number, and *is often ignored* in Chaldean Numerology calculations. It can be the determining factor, in whether your life remains difficult and challenging, or is a life of ease and prosperity. This number can also control circumstances of fate that act upon us, in the form of the unexpected. The Hidden Number can always be changed, if necessary, by altering the name.

# Finding the Hidden Number

When calculating the Hidden Number, you want *the compound number result,* of adding together the root Day Number and root TNN. This is a simple calculation, such as in the example below:

Example:  Adding up the letters in each name you get:

Keanu = **19/1**     Reeves = **26/8**

1 + 8 = **9 (TNN)**

Day of Birth:  Sept. 2 = **2 (Day Number)**

Add TNN and Day:  **9 + 2 = 11**

**11 is the Hidden Number**

Sometimes the total of the single digit numbers does not add to a compound number. If this is the case, follow the rules listed here for the Day and TNN variations, to find the hidden compound number:

1. *If one number is compound and one is single,* you would add the compound number to the single number.

Example 1:

Johnny = **24/6**     Walker = **19/1**

6 + 1 = 7 **(Single TNN)**

Day of Birth:  April  20 = **20/2 (Compound Day Number)**

Add the single TNN and Day:  7 + 2 = **9**

"Nine" is not a compound number, so you now have to use the higher compound Day Number "20", to reach a compound Hidden Number.

Add Johnny Walker's single TNN and his Compound Day:

7 + 20 = 27

**27 is his Hidden Number**


Example 2:

Angelina = **24/6**   Jolie = **17/8**

6 + 8 = **14/5 (Compound TNN)**

Day of Birth: June 4 = **4 (Single Day Number)**

Add single TNN and Day: 5 + 4 = **9**

Nine is not a compound number, so you would now have to use the higher compound TNN "14".

Add the compound TNN and single Day:

14 + 4 = **18**

**18 is the Hidden Number**


2.   *If both the Day Number and TNN are both single numbers that don't add to a compound number,* use the compound INNs of the name to get the higher compound TNN, and add this to the Day Number.

Example:

Anmarie = 19/1   Uber = 15/6

1 + 6 = 7 **(Single TNN)**

Day of Birth:  Nov. 2 = 2 **(Single Day Number)**

Add TNN and Day:  7 + **2** = **9**

Nine is not a compound number.  We now need to use the higher INN numbers of "Anmarie" and "Uber" - "19" and "15".

$19 + 15 = 34($ **Higher compound TNN)**

Day of birth: Nov. 2 = **2 (Single Day Number)**

Add the compound TNN and Day:  $34 + 2 = 36.$

**36 is the Hidden Number**

3. *If the single digits do not add to a compound number, and both the TNN and Day numbers are compound numbers,* these compound numbers should be added together to find the Hidden Number. (If the root numbers have already produced a compound Hidden Number, these higher compound Day and TNN numbers could still be added together to find a *second* Hidden Number influence on the individual's destiny. See example 2 below.)

Example 1:

Uma = **11/2**    Thurman = **27/9**

$2 + 9 = $ **11/2 (Compound TNN)**

Day of Birth:  April **29/2 (Compound Day Number)**

Add the TNN and Day: $2 + 2 = 4$

Four is not a compound number, so now you would add the compound TNN and the compound Day, (you would not choose one over the other).

Add the compound TNN and compound Day:

$11 + 29 = $ **40**

**40 is the Hidden Number**

Example 2:

Julian = **17/8**   Smith = **17/8**

$8 + 8 = $ **16/7 (Compound TNN)**

Day of Birth:  May **30/3 (Compound Day Number)**

Add the  single TNN and Day:  7 + 3 = **10**

**10 is the Hidden Number**

Add the compound TNN and Day:  16 + 30 = **46**

**46 is the second Hidden Number**

*For a business, the TNN of the business would be added to the Day Number of the date the business was conceived, opened "born" or launched, to find the Hidden Number. If the business is primarily owned by a single individual, you would add the TNN of the business to the Day Number of the owner of the business, to see what Hidden Number is produced.*

## Adolph Hitler's Hidden Number

Sometimes Hidden Numbers can have a positive influence on otherwise negative numbers, as is the case of Adolph Hitler, born April 20th.

Adolph = **28/1**   Hitler = **20/2**

**48/12/3 TNN**

His Day Number = **20**

"Hitler" is a "20". This number's influence is doubled, as his Day Number is also "20". Twenty usually represents a person who went through great trials in childhood which could warp the mind and emotions, and make one prone to depression and/or suicidal thoughts. Unresolved old pain can catch up, or continually interfere with one's future, until support through counseling and/or spiritual direction, helps the individual to function in the world.

The description of the number "20" describes: "A man, woman and child seen rising from a tomb". This image makes me think of the deaths under Hitler's order, and bodies that were piled on top of each other in graves. Also this number has to do with "a calling toward a specific or particular life purpose or obligation", which would describe Hitler's elitist agendas, warped vision and obsessive nature. The solution to mitigate the 20's difficult side is written: "this number may bring setbacks, obstacles and delays, until one has learned to look to their higher nature."

"Adolph" is a "28", a number of setbacks, and danger of loss through trust in others. It states: "Individuals with this number show great potential, promise and possibility for success. Twenty-eight carries with it many inconsistencies, and the probability of having to constantly start over with projects, goals and life. Because of these reversals, these individuals should attentively plan and save for the future. It foretells of danger and loss in lawsuits or the law, loss through placing confidence or trust in others..."

The Total Name Number (TNN) for Adolph Hitler is a "48", reducing to a "12". "The twelve is symbolized by sacrifice, and can literally mean becoming *a sacrifice or a victim* in every sense. This number predicts that you may be subject to, or sacrificed for the plotting and self-interests of others, or something you value is sacrificed." The "12" can be taken here in many ways, as the victims Hitler sacrificed, his ultimate plan failing, and as some conspiracies believe, that Hitler was a pawn for other "powers that be", and was therefore being sacrificed for the bigger plan. It is wise to note that "48" has the same karma as "30". Having advanced mental faculties, and how you choose to use them, determines your fate.

Hitler's Day Number "2" and TNN "3" are not in harmony, making his life, career and reputation chaotic, and drawing in the energies of his unlucky numbers. As mentioned, the "20" is doubled in his numbers. The "20" Day number is not supported by the TNN "3". This doubling, and lack of harmony between the numbers, leads to the extreme negative manifestation of "20" and it's meanings. I knew nothing of Hitler's childhood, but when I Googled "Hitler's abusive childhood", stories of abuse popped up, as I anticipated they would. This is common with the number "20". Hitler also mistreated animals. As an adult, Hitler continued to be the abuser, placing "judgement" on others, and commanding their punishment of death. Hitler's Period Number is "9", which is a war-like number, and although it harmonizes with the TNN "3", it does not harmonize with the "20".

Even with such oppressive number combinations, it begs one to ask how it is that he rose to such a high leadership position, and was able to influence so many with the beliefs of his regime. The answer lies in his Hidden Number, which is the "23" (Day Number "20" + TNN "3"). Twenty-three is an extremely fortunate number. It is called the "Royal Star of the Lion." It ensures success, assistance and support from higher-ups, or those in positions to help the individual. It also implies the individual is protected in some way. Twenty-three guarantees success in one's endeavors. It is a single 5, which harmonizes with all numbers, in a general sense. Unfortunately, Hitler's skewed mental vision allowed atrocities that the world could not support, no matter how favorable his Hidden Number "23".

# CHAPTER FIVE

# The Period Number

I f you are born during a particular time of year, you are known in astrology as an "Aries" or a "Taurus", and so forth. This is called your "Sun Sign", and is determined by where the Sun is in the sky, at certain times of the year. The Sun passes through the astrology signs Aries through Pisces, over a year's time, staying for about a month in each sign. Every sign has a planet from our solar system assigned to it, as its "ruler". For example, Aries, which is assigned the time period March 21 - April 19, is connected to Mars. So, if you are born between these dates, the Sun was in Aries, and Mars is your ruling planet. (The Moon and Sun are included as "planets" in astrology.)

The Sun Sign periods and their ruling planets also have a number that relates to them, called your "Period Number". These Period Numbers are assigned to the same length of time as each sun sign period, (about a month long). In our previous example, if you are born during the time of Aries, March 21 - April 19, your Sun sign is Aries, your ruling planet is Mars, and Mars is connected to the number "9". *Your "Period Number", then, would be "9".* You don't have to understand astrology to find your Period Number. Just reference the following chart, as it lists the numbers assigned to time periods of birth.

# Find Your Period Number

Use your birth date to find your Period Number:

| Born between: | Sign: | Period #: | Planet: |
|---|---|---|---|
| March 21 - April 19 | Aries | 9+ | Mars |
| April 20 - May 20 | Taurus | 6+ | Venus |
| May 21 - June 20 | Gemini | 5+ | Mercury |
| June 21 - July 20 | Cancer | 2-7+ | Moon |
| July 21 - Aug 20 | Leo | 1-4+ | Sun |
| Aug 21 - Sept. 20 | Virgo | 5- | Mercury |
| Sept 21 - Oct 20 | Libra | 6- | Venus |
| Oct 21 - Nov 20 | Scorpio | 9- | Mars |
| Nov 21 - Dec 20 | Sagittarius | 3+ | Jupiter |

| Dec 21 - Jan 20 | Capricorn | 8+ | Saturn |
| Jan 21 - Feb 19 | Aquarius | 8- (4) | Saturn (Uranus) |
| Feb 19 - March 20 | Pisces | 3- (7) | Jupiter (Neptune) |

## How Period Numbers Can Help You

This may seem like an insignificant number, but that could not be further from the truth. The Period Number, like the Day Number, *cannot be changed, and therefore should not be ignored.* Period numbers can be used to alter other unfortunate personal numbers, strengthen weak numbers, and support a positive number, by using its colors, gemstones and increasing the number. They can also cause disruption, if your period number is not in harmony with the other numbers (there are ways to fix this). If, for example, you have "9" as a Period Number, you may want to make sure you have no "8s or "4s" in your numbers (see Chapter Six), because you will feel the difficulties caused by this destructive combination. The numbers 1-9, and their relating colors and stones, are described in Chapter Two. These colors and gemstones are used, *by wearing them on your person and next to your skin.*

## Using the Period Number

If you are born under an unlucky Day Number, such as "26" (loss and failure, having to do with taking risks and associations with others), you would want to negate the energy of this number. If your Period Number is "3", which is a strong number,  it could be used to replace the energy of the

"26/8". To increase your luck, you would then use the numbers, colors and gemstones associated with the number "3", and avoid the number "8", and its colors, gemstones and days. Referring to the chapter on "Day Numbers" and "The Single Number Descriptions", the colors associated with the "3" are all light colors of mauve or purple. Secondary colors are rose, and all light shades of blue. The lucky stone for number "3" is the amethyst, and can be used here in its lighter shades. All important plans would be made on "3", "6" and "9" days. The colors to avoid for the "8" would be dark gray, black, dark blue and dark purple.

## Solutions for Difficult Period Numbers

Just as in other personal numbers, an eight or a four can be a difficult Period Number, as well. Using the "4" or "8" anywhere in your numbers is something you have to determine for yourself, based on whether these numbers are bringing you good or bad karma. If the energy of these numbers is proving to bring unfortunate circumstances, then changing them, or altering the energy would be advised. For example, an "8" Period Number or Day Number cannot be changed. Having a name with a strong name number, such as 1, 3, 5 or 6, and increasing this energy by wearing the colors, gemstones, and using the number series of the name number, could replace the energy of the Day and Period Number "8s".

Another way to decrease the energy of an "8" Period Number, is to use the eight's *opposite* Period Number instead. By looking at the following chart, the opposite of Aquarius "8" would be Leo, and the "1" or "4" vibration. It is recommended that you choose the "1", as the "4" will increase the "8" energy (see "Rules for Number 8" in the next chapter). Your solution, then, for an "8" Period Number, would be to wear the stones or colors connected to the "1", and make plans on days that are in harmony with it as well. This would include the colors of golds, yellows and browns, the gemstones amber, Imperial Topaz, yellow diamond, and brown and yellow stones or crystals, and making plans on all "1" days (1st, 10th, 19th, 28th).

Note: The opposite Period Number is also your opposite Astrology Sign:

| | | | |
|---|---|---|---|
| Aries | 9 | opposite | Libra | 6 |
| Taurus | 6 | opposite | Scorpio | 9 |
| Gemini | 5 | opposite | Sagittarius | 3 |
| Cancer | 2-7 | opposite | Capricorn | 8 |
| Leo | 1-4 | opposite | Aquarius | 8 (4) |
| Virgo | 5 | opposite | Pisces | 3 (7) |

## Solutions for More Difficult "8" Numbers

An "8" anywhere in your numbers, can give a melancholy tone to your life, and play out its karma, whether good or ill. Because it cannot be changed, but only modified, having an "8" Period Number can mean that you came in to suffer the lessons of the "8", to some degree, or reap its rewards. (If you have both Day and Period number "8s", you will have to use the opposite Period Number, and increase fortunate name numbers to counteract any negative "8" karma.)

Example 1: If you are a Scorpio born on October 26, your Day Number reduces to a single "8", and you have a Period Number of "9". An easy solution may seem to be replacing the eight, by using the nine, making important plans on "9" days, and wearing the colors and gemstones of the "9" (all shades of red and pink, and rubies, garnets and bloodstones). In addition, you would make sure to completely avoid the colors, days and stones of the eight. However, if you read in the next chapter under the rules for each number, a "9" does not mix well with an "8", and may cause great disruptions and chaos in your life. Therefore, it is recommended that one use something other than the Period "9" when it is combined with "8s". It is in a situation such as this, that the colors and gemstones of the *month,* rather than the gemstones of the Period Number, can help. Since you are born in October, the additional color choices from the month of October, (as noted in the chart that follows), would allow this Scorpio person to wear all the lighter colors of blue and purple (such as lilac) and opal gemstones of the month of October, so as to avoid, dark purples, reds, pinks and dark blues of the "8" and "9". In addition, you can use the colors, stones and numbers of the opposite Period Number of Scorpio "9", which would be Taurus "6". Period "6" gemstones would be turquoise, diamond and emerald, and making plans on "3" and "6" days. Lastly, you could also increase the use of any fortunate name numbers.

Example 2:  If you are an Aquarius, born on February 2, your Day Number is "2", and your Period Number is "8". Twos are usually dominated by eights, and can experience much sorrow by association. Since neither of these numbers can be changed, the solution would be to use the opposite Period Number of Leo 1-4. I would suggest using the "1", as it will enhance the "2" energy. The "4" would not be advisable, as it increases "8" energy. Remember that this is true, only if the "8" is bringing about negative karma. (If the "8" seems to be a positive influence, then experiment with using the "4", as it will add to the "8" energy.) If using the "1", then all colors of the "4" and "8" should be completely avoided. Another option, is to wear the colors and gemstones of the birth month of

February, which would be bright colors, neon blues, and the stones sapphires, pink topaz and moonstone.

In this example, your name should be a strong number that harmonizes with the "2", and overcomes the "8". A "1" TNN would be ideal, as it is in the same series as the "2", however "5" or "6" could be a secondary choice, but not the best certainly. All plans should be made on the number series of your name.

## Colors & Gemstones of the Birth Month

| Birth Month | Colors | Gemstones |
| --- | --- | --- |
| January | Black, Grays, Purples | Moonstones, Pearls, Amethyst |
| February | Bright Colors/Neons, Neon Blue | Sapphires, Pink Topaz, Moonstone |
| March | Rose, Pink, Dark Purples, Violet | Agate, Sapphire, Amethyst, Emerald |
| April | Pink, Rose, all shades of Red | Rubies, Garnets, Bloodstones |
| May | All Shades of Blue, Avoid Red | Emerald, Turquoise, Lapis Lazuli |
| June | Silver, glittering shimmering colors, iridescent white | White or red Carnelian (Agate), Sapphire, Diamond, Glittering Gems |
| July | Greens, Cream, White | Pearls, Diamonds, Opals, Cat's Eyes, Clear Quartz, Moonstone |
| August | Yellow, Orange, Page Green, White | Imperial and White Topaz, Amber, Ruby |
| September | Very pale pastels, Silver, Shimmering material | Emerald, Diamond, Pearl |

| October | All Blues, Rose, Pinks, Purples and Violet | Opal, Pearl |
|---|---|---|
| November | Dark Reds, All shades of Blue | Turquoise, Ruby, All Red Stones |
| December | Indigo, Violet, Purplish Pink - Mauve | Amethyst, Sapphire |

# CHAPTER SIX

# Change Your Numbers: Change Your Luck

ssentially, the only way to change your INN, TNN and Hidden Number, is by changing your name. If you are open to changing your name, please follow my guidelines in this chapter, in order to do this correctly. Simply changing your name, to a positive number, will not create the successful results you want to see. You have to harmonize it with your Day Number, and pay attention to the Hidden Number it creates. (If changing your name is not an option, you can utilize the colors, gemstones and days of your more positive personal numbers, to negate unfortunate numbers...or meditate, using your intention to break any and all contracts and connections to your birth name.)

# Do You Need to Change Your Numbers?

To begin, calculate all your personal destiny numbers, and write them down. Now its time to decide if you need to improve your circumstances, with a name change. The checklist below asks questions which will help you determine if there are problems with your numbers.

| | YES | NO |
|---|---|---|
| 1. *Is your Day Number an unfortunate number?* | ✓ | |
| 2. *Is your Total Name Number (TNN) an unfortunate number?* | | ✓ |
| 3. *Is your Day Number in a different number series than your TNN?* | ✓ | |
| 4. *Is your Hidden Number an unfortunate number?* | | ✓ |
| 5. *Is your first name an unfortunate number?* | | ✓ |
| 6. *Is your Period Number an unfortunate number?* | ✓ | |
| 7. *Is an unlucky compound number appearing more than once in your personal numbers?* (If this number repeats, it is considered a warning, as the negative energies of the number would then be multiplied.) *Or is there an unlucky compound number that is unsupported in your numbers? (see "Rules* | | ✓ |

| | | |
|---|---|---|
| of #4" that follows.) | | |
| 8.  Is there a "15" in your numbers, with any "8s" or "4s"? | | ✓ |
| 9.  Do you have an "8" Day or Period Number, with "4s", "7s", "8s" or "9s" in your other numbers? | | ✓ |
| 10.  Do you have "4s", "8s" and "9s" together in your numbers? | | ✓ |
| 11.  Are you a "1" Day Number, and notice "4s" bringing sorrow or catastrophes to your life? | | ✓ |
| 12.  Do you have a "2" with "8s" in your numbers (and the "2" is not harmonized with your other numbers)? | | ✓ |
| 13.  Is your INN, TNN or Hidden Number an "8" or a "4", when your Day Number is not either of these? | | |
| 14.  After reading the next section on "Rules for the numbers", are there any other problems with your numbers that need resolved? | | |

If you answered "yes" to any of the above questions, you may want to consider a name change (or use the Period Number solutions as shown in Chapter Five). Making a name change will alter the rest of your numbers, and can move your life circumstances into more positive outcomes.

## Changing the Name - Rules to Follow

Changing your name is not difficult, but it does need to be done correctly, so please pay attention to *all* of the guidelines below. I have also done the calculating for you, concerning name changes, by creating a chart with positive name numbers for each birthday. These suggested name numbers will create beneficial Hidden Numbers as well, and can be applied, as long as you pay attention to the other details in your numbers. (See "Name Change Chart" in this chapter.)

*1. Make sure your Day Number and Total Name Number (TNN) are in the same harmonious number series.*

Why does this matter? Having your Day and TNN, in harmony with each other, will make your life experience a smoother ride, and will help cancel out the effects of all unlucky numbers.

What is your Day Number and TNN? Are they in harmony?

The natural number harmonies are as follows:
- 1, 2, 4, 7
- 3, 6, 9
- 5 with 5
- 8 with 8 or 4 (only if you are wanting to keep this number)

If your Day Number and TNN are not in harmony, you can try using a nickname, adding or subtracting letters from an INN, etc. In a worst case scenario, you may have to use a completely different name altogether.

*2. Always keep in mind the Hidden Number, when changing the*

*TNN to harmonize with the Day Number.*

Your Hidden Number is "hidden", because it is often forgotten or overlooked, in calculations. It will be altered, by changing the TNN. Make sure you are creating a fortunate Hidden Number. (If your Day Number is 6 and your TNN is "6", this is great, because these are in harmony. However, "6 + 6" will make the Hidden Number "12", a number of sacrifice and struggle. Although the "12" is a "3", which is still in harmony with the "6", and therefore not as detrimental, a better option may be to use a different "3", or a "9" for a TNN, following the number rules (see #5).

*3. If possible, make sure all INNs and the TNN are lucky numbers, or at least in harmony with the other numbers.*

This includes first, middle and last names, and any titles you are using. Fortunate numbers add good luck to your life. It is easy to pay attention only to the TNN, and ignore the impact of the INNs.

Example:   A first name with an unfortunate INN, such as "Andy" (11), can be altered, by using the name "Andrew" (23), and so on.  Keeping "Andy" would be acceptable if the other numbers were in the "2" series, which would reduce the negative qualities of the "11" (just make sure it doesn't get doubled, and become a Warning Number - see rule #4).

*4. Do Not Leave "Unsupported Numbers" or "Warning Numbers".*

An "Unsupported Number" is any number that is unlucky, (see Chapter 1 "Compound Numbers") and does not have one of the other personal numbers, in the same series, to support it. This is very important, because if you choose to leave it by itself, the ominous prediction of the number will most likely occur, at some point in your future.

An example of this would be a person with a TNN of "12/3", and a Day Number of "1". The "12" is not supported by the "1" because they are not in the same series, so the "12" is left by itself, waiting to take effect. Given that it is the number of sacrifice, I would not leave it as is, waiting for the day when that sacrifice will come to pass. In this case, the name needs to be changed.

A "Warning Number" is any unfortunate number (especially if its unsupported) that *is repeated more than once*. This repetition warns of more extreme or amplified manifestations of the number's predictive meaning. An example of this, would be the number "12", which represents sacrifice. If repeated more than once, anywhere in your power numbers, its meaning could go from a sacrifice as simple as your needs  being ignored, to as serious as an actual death.

*5. When changing the name, consider the following rules for each number:*
(All numbers should use their *own number* whenever possible, except for certain circumstances of the "4" and "8".)

## Rules for Number 1

✧  One harmonizes with "1", "2", "4" or "7".

✧  One is a strong number, and is helpful if you are trying to negate an "8" Day or Period Number influence. If so, *avoid all 4s.*

✧  Ones can use "2" and "7", but these are not ideal, as they represent unsettled conditions or change. If at all possible, "1s" should use the "1" numbers.

✧ The "4" can sometimes crop up in a "1" person's life, as recurring dates, addresses or people, that bring news of sorrow, possible accidents, and unfortunate material or monetary circumstances. Being a fatalistic number, "4"'s can bring in situations outside of your control. If a "1" person is noticing the "4", repeatedly appearing in their life, and it has this type of unfortunate energy connected to it, then I would advise the "1" person to avoid the number "4" in all circumstances, and especially in their destiny numbers. See Chapter 11, for an example of a strong "1" person  attracting sorrow, disaster and possible death, through the number "4".

✧ An exception could be a "4" year (see "Current Year Trigger", Chapter Eleven), when combined with the other harmonious numbers of "1s", "2s" and "7s", in the day or month. Sometimes "1s" can have significant career success, when these combinations come together. This is particularly the case with a "1" day, and "2" or "7" month. This combination is especially beneficial, if the TNN is also "1", "2" or "7". The year, as a "4", would be even more fortunate, if the Period Number is one of these numbers.

## Rules for Number 2

✧ Twos harmonize with the 1 - 2 - 4 - 7 series.

✧   Two is considered a weaker or more passive number.

✧   Two and six seem to bring a secondary harmony to each other (possibly because the six is divisible by three twos). Even so, a "2" individual should strive to include numbers from its own series, first and foremost, in their personal numbers.

✧   Sometimes "8s" should be avoided, if possible, by anyone with the number "2", and deleted from the numbers if using the "2" (the exception to this would be four or more "2s" in the personal numbers, which would overcome the energy of the "8", and quite possibly reap its beneficial side). The reason for this is that the "8" is a very strong number, and will dominate the "2", possibly bringing in much sorrow, heartache, delay, disappointment and loss. Even though the "8" may give financial gain or support to a "2", there is usually a high price to pay for it. An "8" day, for a "2", may be a busy day, with increased business, but the "2" may find they work twice as hard for less money. The "8" will make the "2s" life take on a fatalistic tone, as if at the whims and control of fate, and many painful karmic lessons could come to the forefront. This fatalism could wear down the "2", possibly encouraging suicidal tendencies or deep depression. (If "8" is the Day Number or Period Number, this cannot be changed, and will have to be remedied - see "Rules for

Number 8" below, and the previous chapter on Period Numbers).

✧   As stated, the "2", being a passive number, gains strength by adding a "1", "2", "4" or "7" to the personal numbers. Since the higher octave "2" numbers are difficult (11, 20, 29), they should be avoided if possible (unless they are in harmony with the other numbers and, as mentioned, the individual has four or more of the "2" series in their numbers). It is very difficult to get a name to equal the single "2" with no higher compound, unless the first name and last name are only one letter each (i.e. The name A. J. = 2). It is okay to use a higher octave "2" (11, 20, 29)TNN, if the Day Number is also a "2". This will create harmony, reducing the negativity of an unlucky "2" number, but it's meaning, will still be a theme in the individual's life. Otherwise, use the "1", "4" or "7", depending on which will work best with your other numbers.

✧   Having four or more numbers in the "2" series (two of these being the Day and TNN), brings in great luck at some point in life. Four or more "2s" (four of these being the TNN, Day, Period and Hidden number), suggests a life of great fortune, without major hardships, and will cancel out the energy of unfortunate numbers. People with these concentrated "2" placements will also bring fortune and assistance to other "1", "2", "4" and "7" individuals.

## Rules for Number 3

✧ Three is a strong number, and harmonizes with the 3 - 6 - 9 series.

✧ The "21" and "30" are very lucky compound threes, although the "12" should be avoided, if possible, as it is a number of sacrifice. If you choose to leave it in your destiny numbers, make sure the "12" is supported and not doubled as a Warning Number.

✧ The "3" can be used to strengthen an "8" Day Number, and the "8" can help the "3" attract money.

## Rules for Number 4

✧ Four is considered a weaker number, and harmonious with "1", "2", "4" or "7". Fours and eights can be attracted to each other, and bring fortune in a material or worldly sense, but can possibly require much personal sacrifice as well. If the numbers "4" and "8" are continually popping up together in your life, with negative experiences, one should avoid them as to decrease their unlucky karmic influence. With other "4" or "8" individuals, the relationship could have a tone of sadness, ill luck or terrible blows of fate. If this does not seem to be the case, the "4" should strive to tread gently, heal, nurture and grow relationships with other "4" or "8" individuals, as these pairings can prove to be some of the most loyal around. (It is wise to keep in mind, if the TNN and Day Number are both "4", this brings harmony, but also creates a Hidden Number of "8".) I recommend changing the name, unless you are on the luckier karmic side of the "4" or "8" (in this case, you would enhance these numbers). The Period Number can also help with unfortunate 4s and 8s, unless one's Period Number is an also a "4" or "8". In this case one should increase the *opposite* Period Numbers of "4" and "8", by using the days, colors and gemstones of "1" or "2" Period Numbers, if trying to negate the energy of "4" and "8". (A "1" can be lucky for a "4" Day Number, but a "4" may be unlucky for a "1" Day Number.)

✧ *For all calculations, one should keep in mind that doubling the "4", creates "8" energy. Combining a "4" with an "8", increases "8" energy.*

✧ A "4" should never be combined with a "9" if at all possible. This creates unpredictable energy, with possible violent outcomes.

✧ Fours should never be combined with the number 15, in destiny numbers, as this attracts dark energies.

✧ A Day Number "4" could use "1", as a TNN, as it is the strongest of the 1 - 2 - 4 - 7 series, and creates a fortunate Hidden Number "5".

Here is an example of fours and eights bringing difficult karma into a four's life:

"First Name" = 14/5    "Last Name" = 35/8
TNN = 13/4
Day of Birth: May 22/4
Hidden Number: 35/8
Period Number: 6

I asked this woman if fours and eights seem to bring good or bad luck for her. She said she had not paid attention to how these numbers were affecting her, and did not know. I explained that so many fours combined with eights (fate numbers) and a thirteen (death number), could represent an actual death (she was using a different form of her first name, as well, that equaled a "15", which should not be combined with "4s" and "8s"). I told her the story of the couple who had lost a child (see Chapter Eleven - "Location Trigger"), and had a "13", with fours and eights in their numbers. It was not until the end of the session that it dawned on her, that she had also lost a child, as well. The rest of  her life did not seem to be going well either. Notice that she has a "35/8", twice. My suggestion was she get rid of the "8s". We did an easy fix on her name, by removing a letter, which did not change the pronunciation of it. This changed the last name to equal "32", and changed the Hidden Number to "32" as well.  The TNN became a "10" which, being a one, was excellent for her day number "22/4".

## Rules for Number 5

✧ Five is an adaptable number, and though it can get along with all numbers, it is the most harmonious, with itself.

✧ Although all the "5s" (5, 14, 23) are positive miracle numbers, the "14" has a dual nature. Fourteen gives luck with writing and communication, but it brings with it, warnings for the future, and these can play out through the elements fire, air and water. This can be literally, as in weather events, or symbolically. If your Sun Sign (each sign is related to air, fire, water or earth) or Astrology chart has a lot of one of these elements, you can be at the mercy of this number for accidents or health issues associated with these, since the elements apply to the body, as well (i.e. kidneys related to water; lungs to air etc).

## Rules for Number 6

✧ Six harmonizes with "3", "6" or "9".

✧ If one of your personal numbers is a "15/6", you should avoid "4s" and "8s" in your other numbers, if at all possible, as this can bring dark energy into your life, or take you down a dark path. If it is unavoidable, because the Day Number is a "15" and the Period Number is an "8", then use the opposite Period Number's energy as your main number.

Wear its colors and gemstones, and use its number in important dates.

✧   A two can also be beneficial to a six, as three twos equal six, and two threes equal six, however the six individual should strive to include numbers from their own series first and foremost in their personal numbers.

## Rules for Number 7

✧   Seven is harmonious with its 1 - 2 - 4 - 7 series.

✧   It is considered a weaker number, because of its restless nature.

✧   The "7" is not harmonious with "8", and they should be avoided together in number combinations.

## Rules for Number 8

✧   The karmic effect of the "8" on an individual's life, can go one of two ways. It can be beneficial, relating to karmic reward, or difficult and painful, relating to karmic debt.

✧   The"8" has to do with power and anything used to represent it, such as money, authority, control, or sex. If the "8" is a karmic reward in this lifetime, you will reap the benefit of this. If "8" represents karmic debt, there will be a price to pay for love or success, or you will lack the ability to secure your own power, suffering from difficulties with finances, authority figures and the like.

✧ If you are born on an "8" Day (8th ,17th 26th ) or "8" Period (Capricorn and Aquarius), the "8" cannot be changed. If one needs to avoid a karmic debt "8", then the TNN can be changed to one of the strong numbers of "1", "3", "5" or "6" (as long as the "6" is not a "15/6"), and increased, or the Period and opposite Period Numbers could be used. One should "become" the new number, and avoid "8" days and colors.

✧ To remedy an "8" Period Number, use the opposite Period Number of "1" (but avoid the "2") and its colors and gemstones. In the case of "8" representing karmic reward, it may be wise to increase the "8" energy, by using "8s" in the name, as well as the "8" days, colors and gemstones.

✧ If using eights, be prepared. Eight individuals are children of fate, and at the mercy of life in some way. They can be self-sacrificing, committed, consistent, generous etc., but rarely get this back from others in equal measure. Wealth and success can find them, but the money does not always bring happiness. You may notice there is a conspicuousness about an "8" person that cannot avoid notice from the "gods of fate", making their life controlled in some way, or at the whim of fate or some outside force. For example, celebrities can be trapped by their fame, the paparazzi and their fans. The life takes on a strange quality as if it is not their own, but on some fateful timing and destiny. A lot of times a person is not free to pursue love, because of the fatalistic "prison" of the "8". The "8" individual is usually asked to give up all money and possessions, pay some exorbitant price, or overcome impossible obstacles to be with the one they love.

✧ The "8s" seem to draw in more "4s" and "8s", although one should avoid using the "4" and "8", or "8" and "8" together, if the combination brings negative karma.

✧ *For all calculations, one should keep in mind that doubling the "4", creates "8" energy. Combining a "4", with an "8", also increases "8" energy.*

✧ Twos should always be avoided in calculations with "8s", if at all possible.

✧ Avoid using "8" with "9", as this creates a warlike quality between the two numbers.

✧ The combinations of "4", "8" and "9" should never be brought together in one's numbers, as this might lead to many unforeseen catastrophes or violence.

✧ If one is born on the 26<sup>th</sup> of any month, it is best to avoid "8" partners, as well as any "4s" or "8s" in your personal numbers.

✧ If your TNN is an "8", but your Day Number is not, then I recommend changing the "8" TNN to harmonize with your Day Number, instead.

✧ Finally, be careful not to leave any unfortunate numbers, as "8" can be a trigger of these (see Chapter Eleven).

## Rules for Number 9

✧ Nine is harmonious with "3", "6" and "9".

✧ Nine is not compatible with "8", as this causes the aggressive nature of Mars, to do battle with the oppressive Saturn. It is like butting heads. Nine is already war-like, so you don't want to increase this energy, by increasing frustration with an "8" number, or bring in drastic and dangerous karmic lessons.

✧ Avoid the number "4". Uranus and Mars together is extremely disruptive. Bringing together all three of these planets, with the "4", "8" and "9", in any combination, predicts troubles and disaster.

✧ The dual "18" can sometimes work for success, while at the same time bring negative circumstances into one's future, at some point. If the "18" is harmonious with the other numbers, than it is okay to use this number.

## Name Change Options

In order to make your calculations easier, the following chart can be referenced, to assist with name changes. It lists beneficial TNN numbers, that harmonize with each Day Number. The particular TNN numbers on this chart were chosen, because they produce fortunate Hidden Numbers as well. (I did not give Hidden Numbers for the single number TNN suggestions, such as "2", "4", etc., that create a single Hidden Number, because the compound INNs in the first and last names will have to be added together, and then added to the Day Number to get the compound Hidden Number. *This compound Hidden Number must be taken into consideration when changing one's name, making sure that the higher number is a fortunate number, as well.* Please see the chapter on Hidden Numbers for more information.)

(Note: Although single "1" and "2" are included in this chart, it is unlikely that a name would equal these numbers, unless the person went by only one initial such as "J" or "A. J." Also, remember that "4s" and "8s" are not compatible with a "15".)

Look up your Day Number (the day of the month you were born) on the left side of the chart, and note the possible lucky TNN's to the right, that can be safely used for this day.

| Born on: | Fortunate TNN's for this day: (created Hidden Numbers are in parenthesis) |
|---|---|
| 1st | 2, 4, 13(14), 14(15), 20(21), 22(23), 29(30) |
| 2nd | 2, 4, 7, 19(21), 11(13), 13(15), 22(24), 34(36) |
| 3rd | 3, 6, 12(15), 21(23), 24(27), 30(33) |
| 4th | 1, 2, 10(14), 19(23), 20(24), 28(32), 29(33) |
| 5th | 5(10), 14(10 and 19), 32(10 and 37) |
| 6th | 3, 9(15), 18(15 and 24), 21(27), 27(15 and 33), 36(15 and 42) |
| 7th | 2, 7(14), 16(14 and 23), 20(27), 25(14 and 32), 29(36) |
| 8th | 5(13), 6(14), 19(27), 24(14 and 32), 28(36) - If using 8s - the 17 and 26 would be better than single 8.  Although these numbers produce the 16, they also create a higher positive Hidden Number. 17(16 and 25), 26(16 and 34) |
| 9th | 6(15), 15(15 and 24), 24(15 and 33) |
| 10th | 4(14), 11(21), 13(23), 20(30), 22(32), 29(39) |
| 11th | 2(13),  4(15),  10(21),  13(24),  16(27),  19(30),  22(33),  25(36), 28(39) |
| 12th | 3(15), 12(24), 15(27), 21(33), 24(36), 30(42) |
| 13th | 1(14), 10(23), 11(24), 19(32), 20(33), 28(41), 29(42) |
| 14th | 5(10), 23(10 and 37), 32(46) |
| 15th | 9(15), 12(27), 18(15 and 33), 21(36), 27(42), 30(45) |

| | |
|---|---|
| 16th | 7(14), 11(27), 16(14 and 32), 20(36), 25(14 and 41), 29(45) |
| 17th | 5(13), 6(14), 10(27), 14(13 and 31), 19(36), 24(14 and 41), 28(45)<br>If you want to use the 8, use 17(16 and 34) |
| 18th | 6(15), 15(15 and 33), 24(15 and 42) |
| 19th | 4(23), 13(32), 20(39), 22(41), 31(50) |
| 20th | 1(21), 10(30), 19(39) |
| 21st | 3(24), 6(27), 12(33), 15(36), 21(42), 24(46) |
| 22nd | 1(23), 2(24), 10(32), 11(33), 19(41), 20(42), 28(50) |
| 23rd | 5(10), 14(10 and 37), 23(10 and 46) |
| 24th | 3(27), 9(15), 12(36), 18(15 and 42), 30(54) |
| 25th | 2(27), 7(14), 11(36), 16(14 and 41), 20(45), 25(14 and 50), 29(54) |
| 26th | 1(27), 6(14), 10(36), 19(45), 24(50), 28(54) |
| 27th | 6(15), 15(15 and 42), 18(18 and 45), 27(18 and 54) |
| 28th | 2(30), 4(32), 11(39), 13(41), 20(48), 31(14) |
| 29th | 1(30), 4(33), 7(36), 10(39), 16(45), 25(54), 29(58) |
| 30th | 3(33), 6(36), 15(45), 24(54), 30(60) |
| 31st | 1(32), 2(33), 10(41), 11(42), 19(50), 28(59), 29(60) |

## Specific Warnings for the  13, 14, 15 & 18

Some compound numbers *have a dual nature, meaning they can be beneficial or unfortunate, depending on  how they combine with other numbers.* Dual-natured numbers affect your life through harmonies/disharmonies with your destiny numbers, addresses and other personal numbers. What follows are specific warnings about some of these dual numbers. These warnings are not meant to scare you, but rather to assist you in avoiding the unhappy side of life, that can be caused by ignoring the influence of the "13", "14", "15" and "18".

**13** - The "13" is usually considered a fortunate number. It is represented by the "Death" card in tarot. When "13" is not in harmony with the other numbers, it can play out this "death" aspect. This is especially true, and even more literal, when combined with the "12", "16" or "18" (all numbers with "death-related" warnings in their meanings). If one of these numbers, ("12", "16" or "18") *is left unsupported*, and there is a "13" present, then the likelihood for an unfortunate death of a loved one, or oneself is possible. In the case of the "12", this could represent a death of a sacrificial nature;  the "16" could portend a sudden death; the "18" may suggest a violent or overpowering death. Also, if the "13" is left unsupported, the same can occur.

When "13" is combined with the number "15", in your personal numbers, there will be problems. These two numbers represent "Death" and "The Devil". The "13" reduces to a "4". It is not recommended for "15" to be combined with "4s" or "8s", which attracts the darker side of life. The connection of the "15" and "13" can play out scenarios, such as the individual being attracted to black magic, demonology etc, or attracting dark forces to themselves. This can also manifest as others practicing dark arts against you. It is common for someone with "15" and "13" to attract a partner with a drug or alcohol problem, or other addictive tendencies. This partner is hard to get away from, and may resort to stalking or becoming a threat in some way. In turn, the "15" individual may be drawn to drugs or destructive addictive behaviors, becoming reckless or careless. This combination with "15" and "13/4" can bring loss and sorrow, and it would be wise to change your numbers accordingly. In all other circumstances, "13" is an extremely fortunate number.

**14** - The "14" reduces to the magical "5", so in essence, it is lucky. The warnings with this number can occur when it is unsupported. The "14" warns of danger from natural forces such as water, air or fire. This number is fortunate for dealings with money, speculation and changes in business, but there is always a strong element of risk and danger attached to it, but generally related to the actions and foolishness of others.

The dangers from the elements can be weather-related, or have to do with the individual's actual health. A study of astrology will help with your knowledge of the elements, as related to the human body. An example would be someone born on the 14th of August. In astrology, they would be a Leo, which is a fire sign element. If their name number did not support the "14" Day Number, they could possibly have heart trouble, or complications, connected to circulation, as Leo rules the heart and circulation. Dangers could also come in the form of actual fires. If the "14" is supported by the other numbers, however, "14" is usually associated with the luck of the five.

**15** - As already stated under the number "13", the "15" should not be combined with "4s" and "8s". Any manner of treachery, loss, deceit, dark entities, dark magic, drugs and other addictions can be connected to these combinations, and should be avoided if at all possible. If the "15" is supported, it is a number of good luck. If the "15" and "18" come together, this could mean dark psychic energies interfering in one's life.

**18** - This is ordinarily a positive number, being a "9", but the "18" can play out the violent tendencies of the "9", if unsupported. I have mentioned some of the problems already, under the description of "13". The "18" can bring about violent destruction, whether through man-made or natural means. (See Chapter 8 - "The Mystery of the 18".)

## Examples of Name Changes

If you have followed all of the rules for creating lucky numbers, you will be removing obstacles or finding ways around problems. (Even so, you may still have unfortunate things happen, due to circumstances found in your Astrology Chart, which is linked with Numerology. With positive personal numbers, however, you can greatly soften any negativity that could still come your way.) Following are some examples of name changes that significantly altered the harmony of the numbers, and therefore, the person's luck. Both examples were relatively easy to change. Sometimes name-changing can be difficult, as certain numbers want to "stick" to us, regardless of attempts to find an alternate name.

Example 1:

Tom **15/6**   Fereirra  **26/8**

6 + 8 = **14 TNN**

Date of Birth: August **1**

Hidden Number: **15**

Period Number: **1**

In this chart, the "1", "14" and "15" are all fortunate numbers. The "26/8" in the last name should not be in the personal numbers with a "15". His TNN is not in harmony with the Day Number (although the 14/5 gets along with all numbers, creating some harmony in Tom's chart). This prevents this soul from receiving any benefit of the numbers, or the money and  material advantage that should come from an "8".

Tom chose to change his numbers by using "Thomas" instead of "Tom", and removing the "i" in Fereirra:

Thomas  **24/6**   Fererra   **25/7**

6 + 7 = **13/4 TNN**

Day of Birth: August  **1**

Hidden Number:  **14**

Period Number: **1**

With this change, we have the "13/4" TNN, with the "14". The Death/renewal number with "14" could signal a warning regarding health. Being that this individual is a fire sign (Leo), we would warn him of conditions with the heart, high blood pressure and their relationship to the lungs, etc. However, the "13/4" is in harmony with the Day and Period Numbers "1".

This creates harmony and an incredibly powerful chart, as long as this individual does not use his former name, and as long as the number "4" is a fortunate number for him (see Rules for #1).

Here is an amazing example of an easy name change. (Notice the unfortunate Hidden Number "16", and the unsupported "11", which is not in harmony with his lucky "5" Day Number.)

> (Andrew uses his mother's maiden name "Tuggle".)
>
> Andrew  **23/5**  Tuggle  **24/6**
>
> 5 + 6 = **11/2 TNN**
>
> Day of Birth:  October **5**
>
> Hidden Number: **16**
>
> Period Number: **6**

By substituting his father's last name, this changes to:

> Andrew  **23/5**  Hinton  **27/9**
>
> 5 + 9 = **14/5**
>
> Day of Birth:  October **5**
>
> Hidden Number: **10**
>
> Period Number: **6**

This is now a combination of almost perfect numbers, and complete success, as long as the individual no longer uses the name "Andrew Tuggle". (Note: Andrew has commented that his Hidden Number "16" seems to be an ongoing theme in his life - of projects and dreams falling apart.)

## Strengthening the Weaker Number "2"

As discussed in Chapter Two, some numbers are considered "weak", meaning, they don't have as easy a time with luck, as the other numbers do. The numbers "2", "4" and "7" would be in this category, having a restless or changeable nature, and not offering the stability and hardiness of the stronger numbers. In particular, the number "2" can be weak, unless it is paired with support from four or more of it's own series - and this includes the TNN and Day number being in harmony. This grouping of four or more "2" series numbers, will cancel out the normal negative dominating effect of an "8", and any weakness in the nature of a "2". Four or more of the number "2" series, also brings a fairly harmonious life, with very good luck arriving at some point, in the path of the individual, and usually all at once, such as a windfall. If the Period, Hidden, Day and TNN are all in the "2" series, then this good fortune will be felt equally throughout the life of the individual.

Here we will compare two women born on a single "2" day. In this first example, the last name is a "2". This adds to the "2" energy, but since it is a last name, and considered a family name (see Chapter Nine), it does not add *as much* energy to the "2" vibration as the second example. Having a Period Number of the "2" series would have added more strength, as well.

Example 1:

Karly **9**    (Last Name) **20/2**

**11/2 TNN**

Day of Birth: May **2**

Hidden Number: **13/4**

Period Number: **6**

(See Chapter 7) Location Number: **12/3**

Karly's Total Name Number, "11/2", is in harmony with her Day Number "2". This lessons the negative "11" influence. The "11" becomes strengthened and this person may be known by what she says, or the impact of her words. She may not hold back with her opinions, but is still liked and respected for this quality. This would be a more positive manifestation of the "11", rather than its meaning of a "lion muzzled": "It represents underhanded betrayals, trouble, suffering, opposition and endangerment from others. The person it represents may get into trouble from speaking their mind, or opening their mouth in certain circumstances. In some cases, the person has learned from this number, when it is best to remain silent, or refrain from acting out of anger or cruelty."

Karly also has the supporting "13" and "20" of her series here. Hidden Number "13/4", is the weaker number "4", but a lucky compound number, that is supported by her other numbers, and therefore strong. Because it is paired here with a "9" (see rules for the numbers, Chapter Six), this could create a disruptive state of affairs in the personal life. Even so, the "2" series of numbers here can overcome this, as well.

Karly is a Taurus. The Period Number for Taurus is "6". The "6" is not in the same series with the "2" or "4", but does have a secondary harmony with the "2", and helps balance, to a degree, the "9" of her first name INN. The "9" is not harmonious with the "2" series, and is troublesome with the "4". In this case, Karly would use the colors, numbers and gemstones of the "2", rather than her Period Number "6", or the "4", thereby strengthening the two's vibration even more.

All in all, this person's life would be positive and lucky in a lot of ways. She could have a fairly secure life, with minor issues that may come from the "20", relating to repeating patterns created from possible childhood emotional or physical abuse/trauma. The "20" adult can only begin to heal these by pursuing a spiritual path of forgiveness and love. With four destiny numbers in the "2" series, Karly could expect a significant windfall of good fortune at some point in her life. Overall, these numbers signal a life that is balanced, and destined for as much prosperity and advancement as the individual will allow.

Author's Note: This woman has had a stable financial life, and unexpectedly received a very large sum of money, later in life, that guaranteed her future financial security.

> Example 2:
>
> Jane  **12/3**  (Maiden Name) **20/2**
>
> **5 TNN**
>
> Hidden Number: **34/7**
>
> Location Number before marriage: **12/3**

Jane  **12/3**     (Married Last Name)  **26/8**

**11/2 TNN**

Day of Birth:  March **2**

Hidden Number: **13/4**

Period Number: **3-7**

Location Number after marriage: **20/2, 34/7**

Like Karly, in the first example, Jane has a Total Name Number of "11", harmonizing with her "2" Day Number, and a Hidden Number of "13/4". The difference between these two women is Jane is a Pisces with a Period Number of "3(7)". The "7", is in harmony with the "2" series, bringing an added beneficent influence. Jane also does not have the troublesome 4-9 combination.

The "13" death number is paired here, with the sacrificial "12". The "12" is balanced to a degree by the alternate Period Number "3", and the four numbers in the "2" series overcome any serious connections with these numbers. Jane has her main numbers in the "2" series (TNN, Day, Hidden and Period). This combination can create a life of ongoing good fortune. The suffering of the "8" is overcome here, as well. The "26/8" has manifested as the "8's" karma of reward. The "8" would manifest in its positive power aspect, of money, and/or success and prosperity. The karmic reward "26/8" also brings money through the married name and partner. The "12", may be felt here on a milder level, such as having to go along with the plans, expectations or rules of someone else, in the personal or professional life, or being subject to the desires of the partner. Jane can wear any of the colors and gemstones of the "2" or "7", instead of the "3", "4" or "8", to avoid increasing their influence.

Looking at the location numbers, you see even more in the 1-2-4-7 series! Before marriage, she had four in this series, which is very lucky. After marriage, four also, as well as the location of where her luck would play out, being in this series. The two cities she lives and works in, are "20" and "34", and the state adds to a "20"! She also has the eight brought into the mix, obviously playing out as a number of karmic reward for her in this lifetime, so marriage is agreeing with her.

Since becoming married and taking on her husband's last name, Jane has had a life of harmony, financial security and joy in her career, and relationships with her husband and children. There have been no major traumas or setbacks, she has two beautiful children, who now lead balanced successful lives, her marriage has lasted over 30 years, and she and her husband are still in love and do everything together. She's also financially set for the rest of her life.

If we notice both ladies, Karly and Jane, have higher compound TNNs of "38" and "29", which again reduce to the harmonious "2", so any ill effects of these compound numbers are not felt to any major degree.

## Choosing a Name for a Business

Just like a personal name, business names have their own energy in relation to the business owner. Calculate its INNs and TNN. If these are fortunate numbers, you would compare these to either the Day Number of the date the business was conceived, "born" or launched, or to the Day Number of the owner of the business. If either of these are harmonious with the business name TNN, then you would add the Day Number to the TNN to find the Hidden Number. The Period Number would be found by again using the Period Number of the birth or launch day, or the owner's Period Number. If a business has a "dual number" or unfortunate number TNN, such as "16", it would be considered fortunate, if the owner of the business is born on a day in the 1-2-4-7 series. Especially if launched during a Period Number month of the 1-2-4-7 series. (See my free cheat sheet at the back of this book.)

## An Unlucky Eight, Helped by a One

Here is an example of a woman, born under a negative karmic eight, whose luck was turned around by marrying a "1" partner. This woman was raised in poverty, in an unsupportive family. When she married, her father disowned her. Her husband beat her, and he ended up in jail. She divorced him, in a time when divorce was not socially acceptable. She was labeled, and in many cases shunned, as a "divorced woman", now with two children. She received no child or alimony support from the ex-husband. In time, she met a gentleman who was born on a "1" day. He took care of her children, and wanted to adopt them, but the former husband would not let him. They were married for many years, until the "1" husband died of heart trouble, at a fairly young age. This was the price of her "8", but he left her very well-off, financially, and she is set for life. She has lost him, and since then, two grandchildren, but still has several other grandbabies and now, great-grandbabies. Her health has been very good, and at almost 90 years of age, she still drives herself halfway across the country, twice a year. Even though she has had many losses, her life was greatly blessed by her "1" husband.

First Name **18/9**    Last Name    **18/9**

TNN = **18/9**

Day Number:  **8**

Hidden Number:  **17/8**

Period Number: 6

With her name change after second marriage:
First Name **18/9**   Last Name   **20/2**

TNN= **11/2**

Day Number:  **8**

Hidden Number:  **10**

Period Number:  **6**


The "1" Husband:
First Name  **18/9**     Last Name    **20/2**

TNN = **11/2**

Day Number: **19/1**

Hidden Number:  **30/3**

Period Number:  **2**

# CHAPTER SEVEN

# More on Numbers

There are other number calculations to consider, in addition to your five personal numbers. I will discuss them in this, and the following chapters.

## The Birth Month

The month of your birth has its own number, correlating to January through December, which is simply 1-12. The month number is related to more general matters, than the Day or name numbers. It is used to see what is happening in your life, in a broader sense, and its influence is felt as secondary. If you are born in the month of March, your month number is "3". The number "3" would have influence over your life in a minor, but possibly noticeable way. If born in December, you would feel the influence of the "12/3".

The month should not be added to the Day Number or year of birth, as each of these has a specific purpose and influence, by themselves. Adding the entire birth date is common for Pythagorean and Eastern numerology, but is not part of this particular system of numbers. The birth month will be discussed a bit more in this book, as it is used as an indicator in prediction, when in combination with the other numbers. A birth month number can also increase the energy of your destiny numbers. (In the case of 4, 8, 11 or 12, this should be noted.)

# The Birth Year - Your Pattern of Destiny

Just as the birth month number is added separately, you would do the same with the year of birth. The year you were born sets up your "pattern of destiny", which determines important years in your life, that contain significant events. These events are markers or highlights, defining the pattern of your theme for this life. The subsequent years and events that spring from your birth year number, though seemingly separate, are connected and scheduled to occur, according to your life script.

To find these important years in your timeline, add together the numbers of your year of birth. When you get a total, add this back to the year. This second total is the next important year in your life. Then, continue adding the consecutive years.

Example: Born in 1998

$$1 + 9 + 9 + 8 = 27$$
$$1998 + 27 = 2025$$

Future year of significance 2025.

2 + 0 + 2 + 5 = 9

2025 + 9 = 2034

Next year of significance 2034

And so on...

These years are turning points or markers of important events along the way, and the interpretations of these destiny currents are different, for each individual. They are scheduled to occur, and can be happy or challenging. The possible severity of a negative event can be somewhat altered, by changing one's personal numbers to more positive vibrations (as mentioned in earlier chapters).

An example of this follows, in the life of Elvis Presley, a hugely famous public figure. I calculated Elvis' Pattern of Destiny from his birth year. (Notice how his destiny numbers consist of all "8s" and "9s" - the "18", "27", "17" and "8" dominate his current of destiny - the name "Elvis" adds to an "18/9"; his last name is a "27/9"; his Total Name Number for Elvis Presley is "18/9"; his Day Number, Period Number and Hidden Number are all "8").

## Elvis Presley's Pattern of Destiny

*Elvis' year of birth is **1935**.*

1 + 9 + 3 + 5 = 18

1935 + 18 = **1953**

1 + 9 + 5 + 3 = 18

1953 + 18 = **1971**

1 + 9 + 7 + 1 = 18

1971 + 18 = **1989** (Elvis dies in 1977)

$1 + 9 + 8 + 9 = 27$ (End of the repeating 18)

Beginning with the birth date, 1935, you will notice the last two digits, "3" and "5", add to "8", a significant number, in Elvis' chart of personal numbers. The total for the year adds to "18". If you add "18" to 1935, you get 1953. *This is the first significant year*, as a pattern of destiny in Elvis' life. Again, the last two digits add to an "8". In 1953, Elvis sang in public, and gained popularity. In the $8^{th}$ month of 1953, Elvis walked into Sun Records to make his first recording (the address number is $710 = 8$). The $8^{th}$ month coincides with the dominance of the fateful "8", in this man's numbers. Entering Sun Records was a life-changing decision, marking the beginning of his amazing music career.

If you add the total year 1953, you will get "18" again. If you add "18" to 1953, you get 1971, the next year in his current of destiny, and the next significant date related to his birth in 1935. What happened in this year? In early 1971, Elvis received the honor of "The Most Outstanding Young Man of the Year" by the Jaycees. This award meant a lot to Elvis, and he brought it with him wherever he went. In June, 1971, Elvis' birthplace in Tupelo was opened to the public, for the first time, and Elvis recorded his signature song for his last days, "My Way". The lyrics: "And now...the end is near...and so I face the final curtain..." are very poignant, considering his death was only six years after this recording. The Memphis City Council voted to change Elvis' home street to "Elvis Presley Boulevard". And finally, in the $8^{th}$ month of 1971, Elvis became the first rock and roll singer to be awarded the

"Lifetime Achievement Award", by the Grammy Award Organization. [7]

The last two digits of 1971, the "7" and "1", add to "8" again, and the total year 1971 adds to "18", yet again! 1971 plus "18" gives you 1989. Elvis died before reaching his next destiny year of 1989. (Interestingly enough, in 1989, The movie "Mystery Train" hit theaters. It mixes together three different stories, all connected to a Memphis hotel and the spirit of Elvis Presley.)

The last two digits of 1989, the "8" and "9", add to "17", another "8". The year 1989 added together gives you "27", and here the number "18" stops its recurrence. Elvis does not live to see the year, 1989. You can see the influence of the "18" in this man's life. Also interesting, is that the only other "9" in his numbers (see Chapter 8 - "Celebrities and Numbers") was a "27". I wanted to keep adding "18" anyway to see what would have happened in Elvis' "life". Using the last current of destiny year 1989, and adding "18" gives me the year 2007. In 2007, Elvis' daughter Lisa Marie records "In the Ghetto", a duet with her father, inserting her voice into his original recording. I find it interesting that Elvis' name lives on after him, through his Hidden Number 17, and he records a new record, even after death.

## Steve Jobs' Pattern of Destiny

*Steve Jobs' year of birth is 1955.* If you add up 1955, you get "20". Adding "20" to 1955, gives you 1975, the next significant year in the destiny of Steve Jobs. When one thinks of Steve and his life, one cannot help but think of Apple. Apple was not

---

[7] Elvis Presley Timeline: 1971, by Robert Fontenot

officially formed until 1976, so what exactly happened in 1975? Notice in the following chapter on celebrities, that Steve's numbers are almost entirely the 3-6-9 series. So, it is not surprising, that in the 6*th month* of 1975, Steve Jobs' friend, Steve Wozniak, presented him with a pieced-together computer. June 29, 1975 marks the day that two Steves first got together to change the world. It was the moment of conception for what would end up being the prototype for the Apple I, the world's first mainstream assembled personal computer. Everything followed from there, including Mac, the iPhone, iPad and almost the entire world of consumer tech.[8]

If you add 1975, you get "22". 1975 plus "22" is 1997. 1997 was an important year in this man's life, as it is considered his "comeback". Apple fired Steve Jobs and then entered into a downward spiral. When Gil Amelio took the company over and served as CEO of Apple for a year, he bought Jobs' company "NeXT", and brought back Steve Jobs to Apple. In harmony with his 3-6-9 series, Steve Jobs was formerly named "Interim Chief Executive" in September of 1997, a "9" month. When Jobs took over again as CEO in 1997, Apple's market capitalization went from $3 billion to $350 billion in 2011, worth more than Microsoft and Dell combined, making Apple the second most valuable company in the world. [9]

If you add 1997, you get "26". 1997 plus "26" equals 2023. The "26" is an "8", a fatalistic number, signaling that he would not make this next sequence of years, as the "15" in his

---

[8] "37 Years Ago Today, Steve Jobs & Steve Wozniak Invented Apple", by John Brownlee

[9] "Steve Jobs: The Return, 1977 - 2011

personal numbers does not relate well with "4s" and "8s". If you add the single "8" to 1997, you get 2005, the year of Steve Job's epic Stanford commencement speech, and of course this was in a "6" month - June. He was Stanford's 114th commencement speaker, which also adds to a "6".[10] Jobs died in 2011, adding to a "4". We find a "13/4" in his personal numbers, combined with a "15" - the only minor flaw in his almost perfect number set (see Chapter 8 - "Celebrities and Numbers"). The unsupported "13" and "15" combined can bring the literal translation of "death" of the thirteen.

## A Major Life Event & its Pattern of Destiny

In addition to the birth year, you can add *any year that contains a major event*, and see its domino effect on future years in the same way. For example, lets say you quit a job you held for twenty years. To see the snowball effect of this major decision, add up the year you decided to quit. This total will give you the year of the next event set to happen, that was set in motion by your decision. So if you quit in the year 1998, this adds to "27". Since twenty-seven is a fortunate number, this may be an indicator of a wise decision, especially if your numbers are in the 3-6-9 series. Add 27 years to 1998 and you get 2025. 2025 will be the year to look for an event that will occur, as a by-product of your decision to quit your job. It represents one road or choice in your destiny. Had you decided not to quit, the circumstances in 2025 may be quite different. Perhaps you are able to retire in this year, due to a better career choice. You could then add 2025, which would

---

[10] "Steve Jobs ' 2005 Stanford Commencement Address" by David M. Ewalt

total a "9". This signals  2034 to be the next significant year in this succession from 1998.

# Finding Favorable Days

Adding up the year of birth or the current year of a major event will give you an impression of what is coming in the future years. To find a fortunate *day*, however, *to take action or plan an event* for the immediate or near future, is quite simple:

- *For general purposes*:  Finding a fortuitous day for taking action, of any kind, has been mentioned in the chapter on Single Number meanings. You would simply *use the days that are in harmony with your Day Number series.* If you are born on the 21st of any month, you would plan to implement your desires on all "3" days (3rd, 12th, 21st and 30th of any month). Secondary days for a person born on the 21st would be all the interchangeable number series of "6" or "9".
- *For special purposes*:  The second way of finding a special day, is to add the number of the day in question to your TNN and Day Number. If the result is a fortunate number, then it is a good day. If the result is in the same number series with the day in question, or your own numbers, all the better. Another factor that can be favorable in a more general sense, is the outcome being in harmony with the month number. An example:  Mary Jones, is born on Dec. 3rd, and wanting to know if June 30th  is a good day for her to get married.

Mary = **8**  Jones = **21/3 = 11/2 TNN**

Step One:  She would add her TNN number of "11" to the prospective wedding day, which in this case would be "30", to her Day Number of "3".  11 + 30 + 3 = 44/8.  Her wedding day would have "8" energy.

Step Two: The "44" has the same meaning as the number "26", which says: "Twenty-six carries a very serious warning of destruction, caused by gambling, risk, misinformation, partnerships, mergers and alliances. Not a lucky number." The "44/8" is also not in the same number series with the "6" month June, or the 30th. (Mary would also compare the "26" to her own personal destiny numbers.) This would suggest that June 30th would probably not be a good day for Mary Jones to get married.

# Location Numbers

The location where you live is very important, as it will affect and interact with your personal numbers. It is the place where your luck happens. The important locations are the number of your home address, the city or town number, and in a more general sense the state, county or even country. The home number is what happens in your home, the city, state or county is where you work or interact with the world. (Your street *name number* does not apply, as there are other homes on that street. We are looking for the energy of the building where you reside.  This is the number on your house.) Also keep in mind the effects of any addresses of businesses where you work, or other significant places in your life where you spend time, such as the gym, hair salon etc.

If the address number of your home adds to a "5", this would be harmonious for all "5" people in the home. The home life and all activities in the home would reflect this number. If you live in an apartment, this same rule would apply for your building number. All activities in that particular building would be ruled by it's address number, so all residents would experience the influence from this number. The number or letter of your individual apartment would apply to your apartment specifically. For example, the building address is 5947. This adds to "25/7", a harmonious number, and all residents in that building would be under its influence. If you lived in this building, and you resided in Apartment "1", your home would be under the "1" influence as well. If you lived in "Apartment C", your home would be under the "3" influence, because the letter "c" equals a "3".

## Cities by the Number

The number vibration of the town, where you reside, has an influence on how easy or difficult the circumstances of your life may be, in this location. Building a career, a group of friends or a happy relationship may prove difficult if your destiny numbers are not in harmony with the area in which you live. Although some of your circumstances can be helped by studying Feng Shui, astrology and other available tools, Chaldean Numerology does play a major role in placing you on the best path possible.

Add up the city or town you live in, and see how well your numbers harmonize with that area. Remember, if you have left unfortunate numbers in your destiny numbers, you do not want them repeated in your city of residence. For example, if you have a "12" in your numbers, you do not want it repeated anywhere else, because it could strengthen the sacrificial influence of the "12".

The INN/TNN numbers for several large cities follow:

## Number 1 Cities:
New York City 16, 12, 9 (19); Hong Kong 20, 17 (10);   Reno (19); Atlanta (19); Tucson (28); Boston (28); Houston (37).

## Number 2 Cities:
Los Angeles 13, 25 (11); Washington DC 40, 7 (11); Baltimore (29); San Diego 9, 20 (29); Cincinnati (29); Miami (11); Pittsburgh (38); Stockholm (38); Sydney (19); Taipei (20).

## Number 3 Cities:
Tokyo (21); Dublin (21); Melbourne (39); Cape Town 17, 22 (12); Memphis (30); Newark (21); Lisbon (21); Moscow (30); Jakarta (12).

## Number 4 Cities:
London (31); Indianapolis (40); Cape Cod 17, 14 (13); Bangkok (22); Quebec (22); Montreal (31); Buenos Aires 28, 12 (4); Dhaka (13).

## Number 5 Cities:
Dubai (14); Athens (23); Chicago (23); Nashville (32); Vienna (23); Anchorage (32); Vancouver

(41);  Cairo (14);  Acapulco (32);  Calgary (14);
Casablanca (23).

## Number 6 Cities:
Paris (15); Dallas (15); Raleigh-Durham 20, 22
(6); Hartford (33); New Orleans 16, 26 (15);
Honolulu (42); Seoul (24).

## Number 7 Cities:
Portland (34);  Seattle (25);  San Francisco 9, 33
(15);   Las Vegas 7, 18 (16);   Istanbul (25);
Madrid (16);  Helsinki (25);  Mexico City 25, 9
(16);  Prague (25); Pyongyang (34).

## Number 8 Cities:
Tulsa (17); Glasgow (26); Busan (17); Lagos (17);
Ambalavao (26);  Tripoli (26).

## Number 9 Cities:
Rome (18); Phoenix (36); Brussels (27); Denver
(27); Mumbai (18);  Beijing (18);  Sao Paulo 11,
25 (9);  Toronto (36).

## New Orleans  & Hurricane Katrina

A city's numbers can reflect its history. New Orleans has
INNs of "16" and "26" in its name, and a TNN of "15". The "16"
is symbolized by a falling tower, and carries a warning of some
strange fatality. This came to pass with Hurricane Katrina

flooding the city in the 8th month of 2005, an "8" year. The number "26/8", is a number of grave warnings and disasters. A TNN of "15", is not fortunate when combined with any "8s". The symbolism for "15" says, "This enigmatic number represents attractions and the allure of materialism. It is a number to be careful with, because it can draw in things of a darker nature, associated with black magic, dark entities, an addictive partner and the like. This is usually the case when the numbers "4" and "8" are associated with fifteen. This dark side influence can also manifest in the person represented by fifteen, with the individual focused completely on self and gaining what they desire. They will go to any lengths, or they themselves can become involved with groups or practices with ill or evil intent." It is no accident that New Orleans is a city ripe with voodoo and other forms of black magic. A dark side of the city was revealed, during the catastrophe, with citizens looting stores. The "15" also implies help and assistance from others. Much needed help from military and the government for food, water, shelter and evacuations, was delayed for days. The "15" also contains these words: "It is a lucky number for obtaining financial assistance, grants, benefactors, support, gifts and rewards." Monetary assistance did flow in from concerned people all over the world![11]

## Numbers & Compatibility

Who you are compatible with, in a general sense, can be determined by the harmony of the Day Numbers. However, this does not mean you will not like or be attracted to someone, outside of your number series. You may feel a

---

[11] "Looters Take Advantage of New Orleans Mess, by The Associated Press

camaraderie with those in your series, but a more determining factor in the compatibility of a relationship, is in its fate, and ability to last. This is found by mapping the Day Number of your initial meeting or first date, as well as any major milestones that mark a commitment to each other, such as moving in together, marriage and the like.

The day of the meeting sets the tone for the relationship, and where it is headed. Here's an example: Andrew and I met in 2013, a year ending in 13/4, on a "4" day in October. The relationship was then, under a four influence. The next time we saw each other was on November 4th, where we admitted an attraction. We did not officially go on a date until Nov. 8th. (Already you can see the 4-8 number series in action.) In the 4th month of an "8" year, ending in "15", Andrew broke up with me. We got back together, exactly two years after the day we met, October 5. Our relationship is now under the influence of the number "5".

General compatibilities are as follows:

**1 with 1** - Two dominate forceful people, with their own agendas, trying to merge. This can be difficult at times, so this needs to be an equal relationship, with both getting their say, and the power shared. If the goal is the same, these two can be a powerhouse of accomplishment and success.

**1 with 2** - Here we have the blending of the Sun with the Moon. The number 1 person is going to be the leader or dominate person in this pairing, sometimes stepping on the more sensitive toes of the 2. The 1 will be more focused and set on permanent goals, whereas the 2 can be led more intuitively, going with the flow of life. Twos will be more likely to go along with the plans of the 1, with their focus on nurturing the relationship. Even with their differences, these two bring opposite qualities which are beneficial to harmony and compatibility.

**1 with 3** - There is no stopping this combination. Although different in their approaches, together, they bring many complementary qualities of leadership, pizzazz, success and determination to the table. A happy medium must be found for this pair to find any peace, and a normal life. Differences must be overlooked or tolerated for the greater good of the relationship. 1 is the idea person, and 3 helps them to make it a reality, keeping things organized in a system.

**1 with 4** - This combination is either all or nothing. Both have original unique ideas, and can have an appreciation for each other's minds. The 1 must restrain from trying to control or walk all over the 4, or vice-versa. The one is beneficial for the four in many ways, and helps them see a brighter side to life. The four can be unpredictable in their behavior or actions, and this entertains the one. Either they are a blessing, or a curse.

**1 with 5** - These two can work well together, in the sense that a 5 could help the 1 attain their goals, with practical ideas and know-how. Five can help organize and get the word out about 1s plans. This would seem to be almost a more beneficial business pairing than romantic, but both potentials are here. If intimately involved, the relationship could be red hot.

**1 with 6** - This would be a secret battle of wills. Six would seem to be going along with the plans of the 1, but working behind the scenes to get their way, or at least be noticed! One and six can find love and a lasting relationship, as long as one can be gentle at times with the 6's sensitivities. Six is a great complement to 1, as they take care of the sensual side of things, and make sure the couple look good.

**1 with 7** - A pair that seemingly is aloof or keep to themselves as a couple, but in private they are very bonded. Both are dreamers. Both need private space. And both understand the other's need of this. Together these are two independent people who stay together on shared principles, beliefs or vision. Overall a harmonious pairing.

**1 with 8** - These two can go places together. Both can tend to be workaholics, but the sense of accomplishment is here. They admire each other for their achievements. They are supportive and very dedicated to the relationship, as long as outside interests don't get in the way. The 8 can attract money for the 1, and the 1 brings strength and good luck to the 8.

**1 with 9** - Here there can be many arguments or heated displays of passion. Each tends to stir the other, and must make an effort to appreciate the good points of their partner to overcome differences. This can be a force to be reckoned with, or a butting of heads.

**2 with 2** - A pairing of mutual minds and hearts. A lot of understanding, sympathy and support is in this relationship. It needs a stable influence though, as both twos tend to back down from taking the lead. Both value romantic partnerships. All in all, this is a harmonious combination.

**2 with 3** - Threes are take charge types of people, and without intending to, can run over the two. If the 2 is not in agreement with the 3, then they can feel disrespected, as 3 takes over decision-making, and acts before the two has even caught their breath. If the 3 can be considerate of the 2, and the 2 trusts the three's vision, they can get on well together.

**2 with 4** - Two and four can be a natural pairing, if 4 curbs their tendency to dominate and control. The 2 may seem to easily acquiesce, but just because 2 is the more passive of the pair, does not mean they are unintelligent. They prefer harmony and union. Despite this, these two do get on agreeably together, in friendship, and love.

**2 with 5** - A two and a five can flow together beautifully. They both go with the currents of the wind - the 5 continually adapting and adjusting, and the 2 following intuitive hunches. Neither can explain where they get their information, on what to do next. They just "know". The 2 may feel hurt from the 5's seeming lack of caring, but this is all in perception, not actuality. The 5 will need to be a shoulder the 2 can lean on.

**2 with 6** - They can be close friends, sharing many of the same beliefs or opinions. The 2 can bring down the 6's natural cheerful disposition with sometimes painful emotional depths, the 6 would prefer not to explore. The 6 may not be as loyal to this relationship, in terms of longevity. This would be sad, as these two can help and assist each other in many ways.

**2 with 7** - A natural pairing, with both possibly preferring peace and quiet, and an unstructured creative environment. They have many things in common, and trust each other with their secrets and dreams. There is also much sympathy here, as each can relate to the other's feelings and desires.

**2 with 8** - Not an advisable combination, unless the 2 has at least four numbers in the 1-2-4-7 series, in their personal numbers. In this case, this can be a harmonious relationship, with the 8 being the dominant party. Otherwise, this could be a painful heart-wrenching pairing for the 2 or both. The 8 can give to the 2, in a material sense, but this never really helps the two, as equal amounts of loss occur. For the 8, the price of love is too high.

**2 with 9** - These two are very different personalities; one seeking peace, and one focused on force of will. They come from very different places, but could meet in the middle somewhere if both are willing to make adjustments and appreciate the other.

**3 with 3** - Here are two people, ready to bowl you over with energy, enthusiasm, ideas and fun! This can be a dynamic combination, leading to great success and love. Both appreciate similar qualities in the other, and find happiness in the joy of living and creating.

**3 with 4** - This can, at times, be a difficult combination to bring together. Both have different agendas or paths they long to travel, or conflicting ideas about the way things should be done. Finding the value in each other, and respecting the wishes of both will help this union flourish.

**3 with 5** - The 3 likes freedom to create; the 5 can just want freedom, period. This pair would be good in business together, and could complement each other's abilities. Overall, a lucky combination.

**3 with 6** - This is a very harmonious combination, with shared affinities and likes. Both have very attuned aesthetic tastes, and could have a happy home life. They support each other, and would make great friends.

**3 with 7** - The 3 is outgoing and extroverted, while the 7 is more of a private introvert. Three can walk all over 7's sensitivities, forcing them into situations where they don't want to be. Seven can dampen 3's enthusiasm, having a depressing effect. Three wants the concrete, 7 wants the ideal. These two must find ways to work around the difficulties, by

3 lowering their expectations of companionship, and 7 coming out of their shell more often.

**3 with 8** - A powerhouse combination, as the 3 can clear the karmic path for the 8, and the 8 attracts financial benefits and opportunities for the 3. This pair can make many powerful friends, and have a wide network of assistance.

**3 with 9** - An energetic combination of drive and luck. This can bring a very fruitful relationship, in all areas. These two can be great friends and lovers. Energy, excitement and love can abound. Strong family ties.

**4 with 4** - These 2 lonely souls seem to find comfort in each other, having found a kindred spirit. Both have unique views about how a relationship should be, and appreciate the original mind of the other. Tolerance is needed, as these two can be too much alike.

**4 with 5** - This can be a combination where these two have trouble coming together. The 5 will seem reckless in money matters to the 4. Four will seem too restrained to the 5. Both have their own unique way of doing things, and can be stubborn. They would need help here from their astrology placements to make this a long term match.

**4 with 6** - This can be a harmonious relationship, with the 6 overpowering the 4, in terms of will. Although the 4 will try to inflict their way, they seem more apt to give in to the 6, than with the other numbers. This is a relationship of tolerance, and some harmony, if reason can convince both to see eye-to-eye.

**4 with 7** - This can be a harmonious relationship, if the 4 will not try to control the 7. Both need "me" time. They can have opposite viewpoints, but share a common middle ground, or end up with the same conclusions. There is no reason these two cannot be happy together, if they will allow it.

**4 with 8** - An attraction that seems beyond their control. This can be a difficult relationship for the 4, if the 8 person is living out the karmic debt from the number 8. The 4 can be a benefit to them, or can just as easily make things worse. If their astrology Sun signs are in harmony, they can benefit each other. If the 8 person is living out karmic reward, then this can be a beneficial relationship in many ways. Either way, there is much loyalty here, in terms of support.

**4 with 9** - Usually not an advisable pairing, as the mixture of these two ruling planets can cause much upset that could lead to violence. The 9 would have to have astrology placements that calmed down their tendency toward anger, and the 4 would have to learn to allow the 9 to lead, occasionally. The 9 would have to work on the frustration this placement would cause them, and the 4, on playing the victim. In some cases, this relationship can work fine, depending, again, on astrology placements.

**5 with 5** - This is a natural harmony, and one of the best placements for a 5, as they will receive back the benefits that they give to so many other numbers. This can be unstable from a financial or long-term standpoint, unless both parties are responsible, and want to make an effort to commit.

**5 with 6** - This can be a harmonious pairing, with both having an appreciation for the other. These two prize pleasure, comfort and enjoying life, and will not mind spending money to get it. They flow together nicely, as long as the 5 can provide the companionship and company the 6 will need. Problems need to be communicated delicately.

**5 with 7** - These two will have to be careful not to get so caught up in their own lives, that they go their own ways, or miss each other altogether. They would do extremely well in situations where they would have to travel together. They can be supportive of each other's dreams.

**5 with 8** - A 5 can help an 8 to have a happier successful life, and the 8 can help the 5 find direction and focus. There may be unhappy news or hardships these two will have to face together, but they can have the strength to weather any storm. The 5 helps lighten the mood, of the sometimes over-serious 8.

**5 with 9** - Five wants to find the easy way, and 9 wants to get there yesterday. This is a relationship with lots of energy and change, but at least one of these two needs to learn to slow down, and make sure decisions are being made that are beneficial, for a long term union. Patience and attention are needed with each other, as well as a recognition and acceptance of each other's differences.

**6 with 6** - This is a life lived in beauty, harmony and love. Both parties value partnership and togetherness. If both are emotionally healthy, this can be a lifelong happy union of kindred spirits.

**6 with 7** - Two very different natures come together here, with lessons to learn from each other. The 6 is teaching the importance of union with another, and family, and the 7 teaches the value of a relationship with oneself. If these two can respect each other's boundaries, and give in ways that the other can recognize and appreciate, this union has the potential to be very beautiful indeed.

**6 with 8** - This can be a happy pairing, with the 6 bringing much needed joy-of-living, and a sense of stability to the 8. Any negative karma of the 8 can be alleviated, by the strength of the 6, being willing to stand as a united front on all difficulties. Much wealth and abundance could come to this pair, with a beneficial 8 karma.

**6 with 9** - This can be a happy relationship, if each understands their roles within it. This is the joining of complementary natures, and personalities naturally supportive to the other. Romance can definitely be something natural that is found in this pairing. An overall harmonious joining, on all levels.

7 **with** 7 - These two may never find each other, living in completely separate cities, or they could meet by some spiritual decree of fate, locked away together, in their own private world. They need to meet at a time when both are looking for companionship, for this is a joining of souls on the same journey.

7 **with** 8 - This is not a natural pairing, and could prove difficult. The delicate dreams of the 7 get hit with the cold hard reality of the 8. Much sadness and despair could be the lineup here, as fate simply seems to be outside of the control of these two. Forgiveness and unconditional love, as can be expressed by an advanced soul, is needed. Delusions, addictions, pain and suffering could be the outcome, if the 8 is living out karmic debt. With love, all things are possible.

7 **with** 9 - This is a union of very different temperaments. The 7 is idealistic, and prefers a life of more quiet serenity, and the 9 is full of exuberance and passion. The 9 relies on drive and willpower, and the 7 just wants to flow. These two could come together in harmony, if each is okay with the other having a life independent of the relationship.

8 **with** 8 - This is a powerhouse combination of all-or-nothing. There is not a limit, on the success these two can achieve together, or independently. This is usually the case if

both parties are playing out a life of karmic reward. If one partner is living karmic debt, then there can be much misery for the stronger partner, and much unhappiness.

**8 with 9** - A difficult tumultuous relationship, that can lead to much suffering, loss and frustration. Both parties must be prepared to look at their faults, and make an effort to learn and grow together. Since 9 likes a challenge, this would be the ultimate challenge, being with an 8, for learning, growth and self-improvement. The 9 can, at times, benefit an 8 who is living the karmic debt of the number 8. This is much more harmonious if the 8 person is living a life of karmic reward.

**9 with 9** - This is a doubling of the Mars energy, and although this signifies much potential, it can just as well be disruptive, or these two may find themselves butting heads. There is, no doubt, a lot of energy, and the bedroom life may be one of fireworks. It depends on how well each has rounded the other facets of their natures, as well as congruous traits of their astrology Sun signs, if these two are to get along, for the long term.

# 8 Ways to Improve Your Luck: Summing Up

● Harmonize your Day and INN.
● Use the colors, numbers and gemstones of your Day or Period Number.
● Use the colors, numbers and gemstones of your opposite Period Number.

- Use the colors and gemstones of your birth month.
- Use dates in your number series, when making future plans.
- Find favorable days, by adding the day in question to your Day Number and TNN.
- Change your name to change your numbers.
- Relocate to cities and addresses that are in harmony with your numbers.

# CHAPTER EIGHT

# Celebrities and Numbers

I have always found accuracy, in studying the lives of those close to me. Because I have first hand knowledge of what is actually occurring in their life, it is with these individuals that I can clearly see fate, playing itself out through their numbers. The workings of destiny can also be seen in the lives of celebrities and their numbers. I must stress here that none of us really knows what actually goes on in their personal lives. One can only study what is known of them publicly, or how they appear to be. In studying the lives of celebrities, you will many times find that their numbers amazingly correspond to their life events, such as I have. Unless you know these individuals on a personal basis, though, you will also find some of their numbers remain a mystery, the effect of which, one can only speculate.

# Born Under a Lucky Number?

Some people have all the luck! This appears to be the case with actress Sharon Stone:

Sharon   **23/5**   Stone   **24/6**

5 + 6 = **11/2 TNN**

Day or Birth:  March 10 = **1**

Hidden Number:  11 + 10 = **21/3**

Period Number:  **3 or** 7

Sharon's INNs are "23" and "24" - both fantastic numbers. The "23":  "...ensures success, assistance and support from higher-ups, or those in positions to help the individual. It also implies the individual is protected in some way. Twenty-three guarantees success in ones endeavors." And "24" says: "attracts alliances with those in high positions to help the individual achieve their goals. There is an allure that attracts love ties and amorous relationships, that can also be beneficial." Here is the beginnings of a recipe for success! Her TNN is "11", which is in harmony with her Day Number "1". The Hidden Number is "21", another fortunate number. "It is a number of progress and overall success, achieving prestige, recognition and distinction. It is considered a fortunate number of success." The Period Number "7" is in harmony with both her TNN and Day Number. The secondary Period Number "3" is in harmony with her Hidden Number and is ruled by the lucky planet Jupiter. This is a chart of worldly and personal success. This woman has lucky numbers, any way you look at it. If her palms or   astrology chart showed any unfortunate circumstances, her fortunate Chaldean numbers would override and overcome those setbacks, disappointments or troubles. Lets see how this applies to what we know of Sharon

Stone's personal history:

Sharon Stone's luck started at an early age. She won a scholarship to Edinboro University at age 15, and graduated. Shortly thereafter, she won the Miss Pennsylvania Beauty Pageant. Ford Modeling Agency in New York City decided to sign her on. Miss Stone became a highly sought after model in print and television ads. She decided she wanted to branch out into acting, and for two decades, was cast in several movies, and made numerous television appearances. Sharon's Playboy Magazine spread earned her a spot as one of their "Top 25 Sexiest Stars of the Century" list! She went on to win Golden Globe and Saturn award nominations, for the movie "Basic Instinct." Empire Magazine proclaimed her as one of the 100 sexiest stars in film history. People Magazine listed her in the "50 Most Beautiful People." Sharon won a Golden Globe and an Academy Award nomination for "Casino." Today, at age 55, she has kept her youthful look, and according to her, is constantly pursued by men in their 20's. She has had three divorces and a health issue through all of this, but none of it stopped her from having a fabulous life and career.[12]

Steve   **23/5**   Jobs   **13/4**

5 + 4 = **9 TNN**

Day of Birth: February **24/6**

Hidden Number: **15/6**

Period Number: **3**

Steve Jobs co-founded Apple Computers, when he was 21, and by the age of 23, he was a millionaire. His first name adds

---

[12] Sharon Stone, Wikipedia.

to a "23". Steve had fantastic numbers: 23, 13, 9, 24, 15 and 3. His TNN "9" is in harmony with his Day Number, which is the extremely fortunate "24/6". His Hidden Number and Period Number are both supported as well. There is a "4"   in combination with a "9". These two numbers do not get on well together, as this is the mixing of the energies of Uranus and Mars. This can signal an emotional nature of passionate, angry or violent outbursts and shocking behavior. We also find the "15" combined with the "13/4". The "15" attracts manipulation and dark forces with "8s" and "4s". Otherwise this is truly a harmonious grouping of numbers of the 3-6-9 series.

Peyton **30**   Manning   **24**

3 + 6 = **9 TNN**

Day of Birth: March **24**

Hidden Number: **15**

Period Number: **9**

These personal destiny numbers suggest a charmed life! I do not have to know anything about sports to understand this is a successful person, as there is not an unfortunate number in the entire chart. *Every one of them* is in the 3-6-9 series! The TNN and Day of Birth are harmonious. Peyton Manning, as we know, is a professional quarterback, had a seemingly perfect childhood, idolized his parents and was an "A" student. He broke multiple records in his sport, was honored as the "Gatorade Circle of Champions National Player of the Year" and the "Columbus (Ohio) Touchdown Club National Offensive Player of the Year". Manning was the richest NFL rookie in history, received multiple MVP trophies, has so far attended three Super Bowls and won a Super Bowl ring. In his personal life, he married his college sweetheart, and has two beautiful children. Enough said.

## Love Triangles & Other Trinities

The following three public figures, Elvis Presley, Brad Pitt and Angelina Jolie have the number "18/9", combined with "8", in their charts.

I will begin with Elvis Presley, one of the most influential people of the 20<sup>th</sup> century. *Elvis studied Chaldean Numerology, astrology and the mystical arts,* and was dubbed "The King of Rock and Roll". I have already calculated Elvis Presley's pattern of destiny years in the previous chapter. Here are his destiny numbers:

Elvis   **18/9**   Presley   **27/9**

$9 + 9 = $ **18/9 TNN**

Day of Birth: January **8**

Hidden Number: $9 + 8 = $ **17/8**

Period Number: **8**

The first thing I notice is all of his numbers are "8'"s and "9s". As you know, the "8", if it is acting through the karma of the Sword of Justice, can bring sorrow and many disappointments in love and the personal life. The "8" and "9" together create much discord and upset. The "8", however, gives the individual a sense of being controlled by fate. We can easily see this mirrored in Elvis' life. According to many biographies, for most of his career, his manager, Colonel Tom Parker, "owned" him from a financial and legal standpoint.

Fame trapped him. Elvis could not go anywhere without being mobbed by fans or the press. To avoid this, he would rent out a movie theater in the middle of the night, just so he could watch a movie without being interrupted, and soon developed the habit of staying up all night. He began to take sleeping pills, to help him sleep during the day, and it was believed he developed a dependence on them. His desperate need for privacy became common knowledge, and many today still believe he faked his death in 1977, in an attempt to escape his fame.

I'll share an interesting tidbit here, pertaining to the years I lived in Memphis, around 1992 or '93. While a resident, I met a lot of people who had personally known or had encounters with Elvis. I found this incredible, as Elvis had been a worldwide star, and household name. He seemed surreal. Even so, it became apparent to me, that seeing Elvis around town, had been a common occurrence for Memphis locals. One night, I was at a friend's party, and mentioned something about the rumors that Elvis may still be alive. This got the attention of a man at the party, (it was so long ago, I don't remember his name) who, like other locals, did not believe Elvis had died. He told me a story of how he and another man had broke into the cemetery to see for themselves, and found Elvis' grave empty. Shortly thereafter, the grave site was moved to Graceland, with the mysterious spelling of Elvis' middle name on the stone marker as "Aaron", instead of "Aron". The misspelling is interesting, considering the fact that Elvis studied Chaldean Numerology and was fascinated with the "8s" in his chart. The name "Elvis Aron Presley" has a very fortunate TNN number of "24". Why would he want to change this number by changing his name? Possibly, Elvis did not want to mix the "15" of Aron with the

"8"'s in his chart? Also odd, is that Elvis' was known to lament the death of his twin at birth, Jesse Garon. The name "Aron" was in "Garon", so many find it hard to believe he would change it. Some think it was a way of saying Elvis was not actually buried there.[13] Nevertheless, his father Vernon claimed Elvis had been named "Aaron", after his best friend in Tupelo, Aaron Kennedy, and that Elvis had wanted the name changed to "Aaron" prior to his death.[14] Other theorists believe Elvis faked his death and took on the identity of his twin Jesse Garon. Jesse adds to "17/8". Garon adds to "18/9", and Presley is "27/9". This would give Jesse Presley a TNN of "17/8". The full name, "Jesse Garon Presley", equaling "26", would give another "8" to this unbelievable chart. Having a similar name and the same birth date might possibly be an attractive alternative to Elvis.[15] Most who speculate, simply desire to know the truth about a man they admired, or have an inability to accept his death. They want to believe he escaped to a life of his own choosing, finding the happiness and peace that he so longed for; the same peace he brought to so many.

Money, also associated with "8"'s, eventually became a problem for Elvis. Although he was good at making it, he was also good at spending it, and was forced to go back to work performing and recording during the late 60s and early 70s. Intimated by Larry Geller, in his book "If I can Dream", Elvis was beginning to realize that wealth and fame no longer held any meaning for him. His devotion to his spiritual beliefs created a desire to detach from worldly goods. (Elvis was rewarded in the extreme, materially, and this striving toward

---

[13] Brewer-Giorgio, Gail. "Is Elvis Alive?".
[14] Lacker, Marty. "Elvis and the Memphis Mafia".
[15] Geller, Larry. "If I Can Dream".

an escape into spirituality may have come from the two "18s" in his chart.) Material things lost their value to him as something to possess, and were only worth anything if they were shared. After his death, those close to Elvis (bodyguards, friends and relatives) spoke publicly of how they stopped expressing needs in front of him, as Elvis was known to immediately supply whatever was asked for, or desired. There was a story of a fan who complimented his ring, and he took it off, and gave it to her. If someone needed a car, he bought them one. Or several. Eventually the spending and giving away of his wealth and possessions, and the large cut taken by his manager (along with other personal problems) led him to financial troubles. In his final years, he continued to perform a grueling schedule, although his health was suffering.

"Presley" is the number "27", a fortunate number of "...authority and creativity. This number relates to being in charge, having responsibility, and power and influence over others. The ideas of the creative intelligence will find fertile ground, and produce a harvest. A good number if one follows their own ideas and plans." The name "Elvis" is an "18", which can be lucky, but carries the duality of adversity. The "18" can bring odd misfortunes or violence. The TNN is also "18", doubling its influence. Eighteen reduces to "9", and this number antagonizes the "8" numbers, bringing a warlike, chaotic or dangerous quality to life. Elvis' obsessive fascination with guns and law enforcement reflects this "9" influence, along with many death threats made against him. Add to this, the TNN and Day Number are not in the same number series, causing a lack of harmony in this man's career and personal affairs.

His Hidden Number is "17", a beautiful number describing someone who's name lives on after him, and one whose legacy is associated with peace and love. We see this description in Elvis' frequent acts of charity, his music, his dedication to his spiritual path and his love of Gospel recordings, that were so important to him and the adoring fans that he left behind. Even with all of his wealth and fame, Elvis still seemed to live a life of constant struggle. The number "8", in this case, seems to be playing out its negative karmic aspect as the "Swords of Justice". This can mean that any success this individual achieves in love or career, comes with a very high price. If all the accounts of Elvis' life are true, he paid with his loneliness, his inability to find privacy, his painful and highly publicized estrangement and divorce from Priscilla, his declining health and a shortened life span due to a reliance on prescription drugs. With so many "8's", this man's life was not his own.

Brad   9   Pitt   **17/8**

9 + 8 = **17/8 TNN**

Day of Birth:  December **18/9**

Hidden Number: **17/8**

Period Number: **3**

Actor Brad Pitt's numbers are another example of the stormy combination of "8" and "9", but the "8", in this case appears to be on the positive side of "Justice's Rewards", rather than the "Swords of Justice" that Elvis often experienced. As we know it, Brad has a beautiful family, a successful career and seems to be living the life, others only dream about. The "17" is tripled in this man's destiny chart. Any compound number, showing up more than once, is amplified. With three "17s", his living examples of peace and love, will most likely be what is remembered, as the predominant legacy of this man's life. Like Elvis, Pitt is well known for his humanitarian acts and charitable giving, which are the epitome of the "17" energy of love and peace. He founded the "Jolie-Pitt Foundation", to aid with humanitarian causes[16], is a supporter of the "One Campaign", fighting aids and poverty[17], and  of same-sex marriage[18], to name a few. Pitt and his partner Angelina Jolie publicly refused to be married, until everyone else could be lawfully married.

Brad's "18/9" Day Number is not in harmony with his three "8's". It is not, however, doubled as in Elvis' chart, and is in harmony with the first name Brad, also a "9", and the Period Number "3", the lucky Jupiter number. Even so, the chaotic and warlike nature of a Mars "9" does not sit well with the hard lessons of the Saturn "8". This could create conflict, controversy and lack of peace, in his personal or professional life.

His Period Number "3" is expansion in all areas, which means the good and the bad gets bigger. It also adds an ability to communicate in all forms, connect with others and bring his desires, visions and dreams into reality, to share with the world. Threes want to rule, and with this strong Period number, Brad rules the big screen and his industry. The "3" also acts to tone down the "9" war nature somewhat, by giving it an outlet through his craft, with such films as "Fight Club"

---

[16]  Green, Mary. "Brad and Angelina's New Year's Resolution: Help Cambodia".*People*.

[17] Shari Scorca. "Bono, Brad Pitt Launch Campaign For Third-World Relief". MTV News.

[18] Ted Johnson. "Pitt takes a stand against Prop 8". *Variety*.

and the like. I don't recall ever seeing Brad in a "weak" film, or anything without a major message attached to it.

With all of the powerhouse "17/8s" acting on the good side of karma, Brad would most likely make an incredible amount of money in this lifetime. But is it all worth it to Mr. Pitt? Does he own his life, or is he forever trapped in the "role" that fans and the press have created for him? Although many of us might want to trade places with him, does he really have the freedom, happiness or whatever it is he truly wants from life? This is a question only Brad Pitt himself can answer. Let's look at his partner:

Angelina   **24/6**   Jolie   **17/8**

6 + 8 = **14/5 TNN**

Day of Birth: June **4**

Hidden Number: **18/9**

Period Number: **5**

Brad and Angelina have both the "18/9" and "17/8" in common. Her first name, a "24/6", is a number found in many successful people's charts. The fortunate "24" gives potency to Angelina's chart because her first name is used more often than her last name. One simply says, "Angelina", and most know of whom we are speaking. Even though her TNN is a "5", a magical number that gets along well with all other numbers, the ideal name number would be in the 1-2-4-7 series, to harmonize with her Day number "4". This signals some disharmony in her personal affairs, but it is still beneficial, and we see the magical quality of her life and stardom, having not one, but two 5s in her destiny chart.

"Jolie" is a "17/8", and like Brad, Angelina will be known

as an agent for love and peace. She has been a great initiator in her charitable works, and is the "Goodwill Ambassador" for the United Nations High Commissioner for Refugees[19]. She is likely to make money, and will be remembered after her death.

The "14/5" warns of dangers from the elements, and this can apply to the body as well. Being a Gemini, Angelina may need to guard against problems with the lungs, respiratory system or any area of the chest or breasts. The "14" makes her excel as a communicator, especially in writing, public speaking, oration and a grasp of language, as it carries the power of command of the creative arts. We see this in her acting ability, but it makes me wonder if she has a book inside her head, waiting to be written, or a future autobiography. (Author's Note: As I write the previous sentence, I decide to look up this possibility. What I found, is that she has, in fact, been busy with several books!)

Like Elvis and Brad Pitt, Angelina has "8s" mixed with "9s", in her destiny numbers. Specifically an "18/9", which as we know, brings out the possible war-like tendencies of the "9". Angelina also has 4 - 8 -9 combination. This trinity is a mixing of the planets Uranus, Saturn and Mars, which can be extremely volatile. It leads to hard lessons due to a propensity for attracting anger, enemies and aggression, or being known for having, at times, an uncontrollable, angry or aggressive nature, thus making enemies. Her "18" indicates possibly an outlet into some form of aggressiveness, an interest in martial arts, weaponry or warlike tendencies, or these things being attracted into her life. It would not surprise me if she secretly

---

[19] "Angelina Jolie named UNHCR Goodwill Ambassador for refugees". UNHCR.

collects guns or some kind of weapon, such as was seen in Elvis' destiny chart, or has a hidden fascination with the police or military. The "18" as a Hidden Number can also signal possible danger related to one's death. (We explore the "18", "4", "8", "9" connection in Ronald Reagan's Chart, later in this chapter.)

One does not think of the meeting of Brad and Angelina (or "Brangelina" as the press has named them) without remembering Brad's previous wife in this public love triangle, Jennifer Aniston. As a beautiful, talented and much-admired woman in her own right, I am sure she is tired of being associated with Brad and Angelina, by press coverage that does not seem to let up, but the numbers of all three individuals are fascinating all the same. The astrology between Brad and Angelina seems more compatible than with Jennifer and Brad, and I was interested to see if her numbers showed these differences as well.

Jennifer **32/5**     Aniston   **26/8**

5 + 8 = **13/4 TNN**

Day of Birth: February **11/2**

Hidden Number: **24/6**

Period Number: **8**

Like Sharon Stone, Jennifer has both the "23" (related to the 32) and the "24" (as her Hidden Number), setting the stage for a life of success. Her first name INN, "32/5", says " Thirty-two is called "The Paths of Wisdom", and is a fortunate number, with the magical power of its root number five. Its karma is similar to "14" and "23", but this number has to do with groups of people, communities, countries or society as a whole". Jennifer's hairstyles, fitness routines and clothing style have influenced many women's choices all over the world.

Thirty-two is like a double whammy, carrying the talents of the "14" with mastery of oratory and speech, required for acting, and the help from those in high places of the "23". The "14" also gives possible health warnings. Like Angelina, Jennifer is an astrology "air" sign. Aquarius rules the arteries, shins, calves and circulation of the blood. Jennifer is known to be an ex-smoker, and was seen holding a cigarette in public photos. Although it is Gemini which rules the lungs, it is known that more people die from circulatory conditions, such as heart attacks or strokes, due to smoking, than cancer or lung disease. Nicotine and carbon monoxide seem to be the biggest problems. It would not be a good idea for her to start smoking again. The "32", however, is a higher vibration of the "14" and may therefore cancel out any negative health issues for her, but we have to pay attention to the number "8", the number of fate, being doubled in this chart.

Her last name "Aniston", although a money number, carries a high price tag with it. Being a "26/8" it can be unlucky for partnerships. According to the press, Jennifer seems to be having repeatedly bad luck with "keeping a man". To avoid the "26", she would have almost been better off taking "Pitt" for the last name in her former marriage, as the "17" is preferable to the "26". Since her Day Number is a "2", it is dominated by the "8", and subject to many struggles, pain and hardship (her price for love, money or success may be high), even if the "8" seems to be representing karmic reward in her life. This could also be contributed to the highly lucky "24" and "32" carrying her. Ideally, though, dropping the "26/8" altogether would be best, for three reasons. As an "8", it can create incredible sorrow and hardship for the "2", it is a difficult number in the area of relationships or partnerships, and it doubles the energy of her Period "8". It is interesting how "2s" can repeatedly attract the number "8", or people with a lot of "8s" or "4s". At times, the "8" can be financially or worldly helpful to a "2", but there will often be the pain, humiliation, obstacles, loss and depression, that comes from combining a "2" to an "8" (unless there are four or more numbers in the "2" series). It is interesting, and unfortunate, how being connected to Brad Pitt (who is dominated by the "8"), had such a hurtful and lasting influence on this woman's life, and perceived reputation. Jennifer's Day Number "11/2" is compatible, however, with the TNN "13/4". (Since "4s" together with "8s" increase both number's fatalism, and negative characteristics, this would be another reason to eliminate the "8" in "Aniston".) The "2" and "4" together, create harmony in her career, and the "13" is often found in the charts of successful people. Jennifer's Hidden Number also helps her chart tremendously, as it is a "24/6". This can be a guarantee for success, and combined with the "8s", the individual could earn substantial amounts of money. The "6" is a strong number, and supports the "8".

Her Period Number "8", found here in its negative expression, during the time period of Aquarius, indicates, again, the areas of fate, power and money. This Period "8" increases the influence of the "26/8" last name, and the "13/4" TNN. If Jennifer's personal life is one of pain and disappointment, she would be wise to adopt the colors, gemstones and number of the opposite sign to Aquarius, which would be the Leo number "1", in addition to the colors of "2" (her TNN) and "7", which are all in harmony. This would greatly improve the happiness of her personal life, and make her life feel more like her own, and under her control.

Altering the influence of the Aquarius "8" may also help Jennifer in the area of partnerships, bringing us to an alternate solution, which would be to drop the name "Aniston" and take on a more fortuitous married name.

## Sacrifices to the Gods: Marilyn Monroe & Princess Diana

As with most of this book, I feel like this chapter is writing itself. I had chosen Marilyn Monroe and Princess Diana for this chapter, and their names just happened to be in sequential order, before I realized the similarities between these two women. Mainstream media has posted widely about the parallels. Both were blue-eyed blondes, married on the 29th to men twelve years older, and died at the age of thirty-six. Both were born on "1" days, and died on "4" days. Diana died on August 31st, and Marilyn on the 13th. (You may recall from a previous chapter, that the number "4" can sometimes be recurring in a "one" person's life, and can show up as the harbinger of hardship, disappointment and sometimes death.) Elton John dedicated a song to both women, using the same melody, but changing the lyrics. Marilyn was said to have called herself the "Queen of Diamonds". Diana was known as the "Queen of Hearts".

Birth name: Norma **19/1** Jeane  **17/8** Mortenson

Modeling name: Jean **19/1** Norman  **24/6**

Modeling name: Mona **17/8** Monroe **30/3**

Almost Screen Name: Jean  **12/3** Adair  **9**

(It is nteresting how "Mona Monroe" had the same numbers as "Marilyn Monroe", and the other names created similar numbers, such as "12," "8" and "13". )

Norma **19/1**    Jeane **17/8**    Baker **12/3**

1 + 8 + 3 = **12 TNN**

Hidden Number: **13**

Marilyn = **17/8**    Monroe = **30/3**

8 + 3 = **11/2 TNN**

Day Number: June **1**

Hidden Number: **12**

Period Number: **5**

I will begin with the name "Marilyn Monroe", first. In Marilyn's chart, we have the lucky numbers of "30", "1" and the magical "5". The "17/8" would normally be considered fortunate. It was, in the sense that this woman was in a position to make money, or attract those with money, and her name is remembered after her death. The "8" is not fortunate, however, with her "2" TNN. An "8" with a "2" brings hardship and pain, and the cost of any benefit of the "8" is not worth the price. Marilyn, although at superstar status, was one of the lowest paid actresses in Hollywood.[20] Her life was a continual emptiness of the soul. It is common knowledge that she was known to be an unhappy woman, cut off from others, monitored by those controlling her career and life, and suffering from psychological problems, that some have attributed to possible mind control by her managers. Others credit this to her difficult and abusive childhood.

---

[20] Mazzulo, Yvonne P. (August 4, 2012). *Fifty Facts You Don't Know About Marilyn Monroe. Examiner.*

Her TNN "2" and Day Number "1" are in harmony, being from the same series. Her Period Number "5" is in general, compatible, and a magical number for success. The thing that stands out here is the "12" Hidden Number. It is unsupported, and thus signifies a life of sacrifice. This woman's choices are not her own, as plans are always forsaken for the interests and demands of others. The "12" here, can eventually take on the meaning of becoming an actual sacrifice.

As "Norma Jeane Baker", (...and my question is, was she still using this name privately?...) she has the "19", a higher version of the "1", and the "17" and "12" again. The "12" is doubled and unsupported which is a grave warning for the future. (Oddly enough, as is often the case, she could not escape the "12" as it became her Hidden Number with the name change to MM.) NJB's Hidden Number is "13". This brings a "4" into her numbers, which sometimes creates problems for a "1", and increases the influence of the "8". Her childhood reflects the pain of the "4" and the double "12". She was abandoned by her biological father and mother, and abused in orphanages and foster homes. It also combines the "13" death number, with the "12" sacrifice number.

The name "Norma Jeane Baker" does not harmonize with the Day Number. Her life may have appeared better in many ways as "Marilyn", but she still did not have control over what happened to her. Sadly, this woman did not find the happiness that one would think should have been hers, with so much fame, charisma, beauty, brains and talent.

*Marilyn Monroe has a TNN of "2". Her Day Number is a "1".*
*Her first name is an "8". In the rules of numbers, "2s" tend to*
*attract "8s" into their lives, and "1s" attract "4s". These are*
*usually precursors of pain, sorrow and difficulties. She was*
*born in 1926 (the last two numbers adding to "8"), on a "1" day.*
*She died in 1962, in the 8<sup>th</sup> month, on a "4" day, with again, the*
*last two numbers adding to "8". Note: Although the "4" may*
*bring possible hardship to the "1", the "1" can, on the other hand*
*bring good fortune to the "4".*

Her brother, Earl Spencer, summed up her life and
influence, when he described Princess Diana of Wales as a
"symbol of selfless humanity", and "the most hunted person of
the modern age."[21] She is known by many names publicly, and
it is this incredible variety of titles and nicknames, that is not
only unusual, but shows her impeccable bloodlines, and the
level of worldwide notoriety this woman inspired. It also
makes it difficult to calculate her destiny numbers, as all of
these  different names/nicknames were having an affect on
her life.

*Married:*

Princess **30** Diana **12** of **15** Wales **18**

Princess  **30**  Diana **12**

Princess **30**  Di **5**

TNNs: **21, 6, 8**

Day of Birth: July **1**

Hidden Numbers: **22, 43, 36**

---

[21] New York Times. "Brother's Eulogy for Diana 'The Very Essence of
Compassion'.

Period Number: **2**

*Divorced:*

Diana **12**   Spencer **31**

Lady **9**   Diana **12**

Lady **9**   Diana **12**   Spencer **31**

Lady **9**   Di **5**

TNNs: **7, 12, 16, 14**

Hidden Numbers: **44, 13, 17, 15**

(Several other titles could be added to this list: The Queen of
Hearts, The Princess of Hearts, HRH, Her Royal Highness,
Duchess of Rothesay, Duchess of Cornwall, Countess of
Chester, Baroness of Renfrew, The Honorable Diana Frances
Spencer, Lady Diana Frances Spencer and Her Royal Highness
The Princess of Wales, but for the purposes of Chaldean
Numerology, I will use here, the names, under whicht she was
most commonly known.)

In order for simplicity I will start, by separating out the
most popular names she used while married, and then look at
how her names changed after her divorce. First and foremost,
her Day number is "1", and her Period Number is "2". Neither
of these can be changed, so the names should coincide with
these. She would be addressed with the title of "Princess" as
the wife of the Prince, and the INNs are "5", "12", "15", "18"
and "30", with the Hidden Numbers "22", "36" and "43". Her
TNNs are "6", "8" and "21". "Princess Diana of Wales" is a
harmonious name in itself, being composed of all numbers in
the 3-6-9 series, and creating a TNN of "21/3", but does not
harmonize with the Day Number "1". "Princess Diana", again a
name in the 3-6-9 series, with a TNN of 6, does not

harmonize with the Day or Period Numbers "1" and "2". This immediately shows a personal life that is not in accord with her worldly one. "Princess Di", a nickname given by the media, creates a TNN of "8", bringing in the number of fate, and a life subjugated to it. The "8" indicates sorrow, pain and difficulties with the Period Number "2". Her INN "12" indicates her life and personal desires being sacrificed for the demands of her station in life, with its expectations, and rules of decorum, duties and responsibilities, as well as the burden of being the constant apple of the media's eye.

We can see the manifestation of her first Hidden Number "22", which mirrors her experience of married life as part of the royal family, her problems with the Queen, disillusionment in a marriage based on responsibilities, instead of love, and the lack of privacy being in such a lofty position required. The "22" is represented by: "an honorable person who lives in a state of enjoyment, based on false beliefs or hopes; a state of illusory happiness, when one may actually be surrounded by fools. He can be fooled by others, or lured into danger, remaining unaware of other's foolishness, until it is too late. This person can also make bad decisions, due to the influence of others."

Her second Hidden Number "43" states: "Forty-three is not a fortunate number. It is symbolized by the energy of power plays, stirring up opposition, revolutions, conflicts, defeats and failures."

In all of these numbers together, we have paired the "4", "8" and "9", which is a tumultuous combination, creating the possibility of much unhappiness, chaos, conflict and controversy.

After Diana's divorce, she still held the title "Diana, Princess of Wales", unless she decided to remarry. She was stripped of the title "Her Royal Highness" by the Queen. In the press, she began to be called "Lady Diana", "Lady Di" and "Lady Diana Spencer." Here, the numbers take a turn for the worse, combining the "12", "13", "15", "16", "17", "44" and "31/4". She has "4s" and "8s" with "15", the death number "13" with the sacrifice number "12", the "4", "8" and "9" together, and the name "Lady Di" being the homophone of "Lady die". Her "12" TNN is doubled by the first name INN "12". It remains Unsupported by her Day Number. Her apartment numbers at Kensington Palace were "8" and "9". Overall, an eventually disastrous mix of personal destiny numbers.

*"Princess" and "Lady" were calculated for Diana, as these would remain lifelong titles. A temporary title for an individual would not be calculated, such as "Mayor" or any title subject to a term.*

# Mystery of the 18

Some numbers have a dual meaning, as we have seen in the Chapter on Compound Numbers. Eighteen is one of those numbers, with strange qualities about it. "The Moon" tarot card, that represents this number, is often interpreted to mean a mystery, the unseen or hidden. The "18" will not prevent success, as its root number "9" is a lucky number, but this is a dual nature number, which can be both fortunate and unfortunate. Here I present an example of a person with the "18" for a Day Number.

A friend of mine called me a while back, and asked me to look at the numbers for her husband's favorite author, Hunter

S. Thompson. The successful writer had apparently killed himself, and my friend could find nothing in his numbers to refer to his suicide. Here is what I found:

Hunter  **27**  S.  **3**  Thompson  **43**

$9 + 3 + 7 = 19$ **TNN**

Date of Birth: July **18**

Hidden Number: **10**

Period Number: **2**

Mr. Thompson had the positive numbers "27", "19", "18" and "10". These promise to bring in some success into the life of the individual. His TNN "19" is not in harmony with his Day Number "18", therefore the "18" is an Unsupported Number, just dangling there waiting to play itself out. Because it is unsupported, the negative side of the number will be felt, in some manner or manifestation. He also had the unfortunate "43" which, like the "18", is unsupported. The Hidden Number is a "10", which means the individual's life will be known, or his course determined by his own hand.

I asked my friend if this man had, by chance, shot himself. She said, "Yes." The "18" says: "...danger from the elements such as storms, danger from water, fires and explosions." The word "explosions", to me,  can be related to guns or the manmade. His Hidden Number "10" suggests to me that *he decided* the hidden action to be taken (he is the one who shot himself), and "18" - "The Moon" - represents things hidden from view. These hidden things could represent his thoughts about suicide, or something secret done in private. I then asked her if he had shot himself in the head, *and in particular, the mouth*. She said, "Yes." This number also states: "Eighteen is symbolized as a moon emanating the reflected light of the sun, with drops of blood falling into the opened mouths of a wolf and dog, and a crayfish coming out of the water below them." Here is a quite graphic image of blood in the mouth.

I do not strive to shock or scare with this example, or with this book. I am a realist, and cannot deny that wonderful things, and truly horrific things are happening in the world every day. To deny or ignore the unpleasant, and not take appropriate action, may unnecessarily subject you  to its influence.

## Elvis Presley & the 18

Another example of the strangeness of the "18", was in our earlier example of Elvis Presley's Birth Year Number. The "18" was doubled and unsupported in his destiny numbers, and repeated itself in his year numbers. It was also combined with the fatalistic "8". Elvis died when the number "18" no longer showed up in his destiny year calculations.

If one knows anything about the details of Elvis' life, and reads the meaning of the "18", it is easy to see how this number applies to the events and relationships this man experienced. There is a conspiracy rumor that Elvis did not die in his bathroom, but was shot in the head. There are many speculations surrounding his death, due to a corpse that did not share his facial characteristics, and many things that did not add up. I would like to leave it here, as we know it, that Elvis died at Graceland, just as was reported, and we will let him rest in peace.

# A Virus is a Virus

Ebola   **9/18**   Virus   **9/ 18**

$9 + 9 =$ **18 TNN**

As of this writing, the Ebola Virus is of great concern. Its pattern of disease, is to begin with a fever (the number "9" and Planet Mars is related to fevers), and in its more drastic stages, internal bleeding leading to bleeding from the eyes and possibly ears and nose.[22] Ebola Virus is a triple "18".

## Ronald Reagan & the 18, 4-8-9

Ronald   **22**   Reagan   **17**

**12 TNN**

Day of Birth: February **6**

Hidden Number: **18**

Period Number: **8**

I want to present another example of the "18" as a Hidden Number, along with the mixing of the numbers "4", "8" and "9". Reagan was an interesting character. He began as a sportscaster, followed by a career as an actor, and then President of the United States. In Reagan's numbers, the first thing I notice is the "8" Period Number, the "17/8" last name and the "22/4" first name. Here we have an "8" and "4" theme, the fatalistic numbers, and a person's life in the hands of that fate. In the case of Mr. Reagan, we can concur that the "4s" and "8s" were bringing him good karmic fortune. The "17"

---

[22] Mayo Clinic Staff. "Ebola Virus and Marburg Virus Symptoms".

amplified here by the additional "4" and "8", guarantees this man's name will live on after him.

Unlike Elvis Presley, Reagan's TNN (12/3) and Day of Birth (6) are in harmony. Therefore, the "12", which would normally signify sacrifice, is negated to a degree, and the positive qualities of the "3" are felt. In turn, this individual's personal and career affairs would be harmonious. Three people want to be in positions of authority, so this individual had big dreams for himself. The "18/9" is also harmonious with these numbers. We remember from the previous example of Hunter S. Thompson, that the "18" can suggest some type of violence of the "9". The "18" played out with Reagan being shot in an assassination attempt. (True to the "18", the first shot missed, and hit the White House Press Secretary *in the head.* Amazingly, Reagan was only hit by the 6th and final bullet (6 in harmony with the 12/3), and survived this incident, due to the harmony of his numbers. The provocation is, the "4", "8" and "9", brought together here in his destiny numbers. If you remember from Chapter 6, under "Rules of Numbers", joining these three numbers attracts disasters and accidents. With the "18", you have the gunfire or manmade explosives, combined with the "4" and "8" related to acts of fate. We also have the sacrifice number "12".

I do not want to imply, or suggest here, that anyone who has an "18" in their numbers is going to be subject to some type of gunfire or violence, but it is worth noting in destiny numbers, where we have unresolved problems, and the "18" is present. If you continue to research Reagan's incredible life and career, you will see his numbers playing themselves out in amazing synchronicity.

# Other Celebrities

Tiger   **15/6**   Woods   **27/9**

TNN: **15/6**

Day of Birth:  December **30/3**

Hidden Number: **45/9**

Period Number: **8**

Tiger Woods is one of the most successful golfers of all time, and one of the highest paid athletes in the world.[23] He was a child prodigy as well, winning many awards.[24] He has fantastic numbers in the 3-6-9 series, including two fifteens, a "27", a "30" and a "45". This is pretty much hard to beat. The "8" Period Number suggests fate, and the acquisition of money. The only problems here are the "15", combined with an "8", bringing addictions and dark side influences and temptations, and the "8" with a "9", pulling in the energy of chaos and destruction. These can be seen in his publicized marital indiscretions and divorce which lost him sponsorships,[25] leading to a loss in his form, and ending his winning streak. You can see clearly, in his public confession, the dark energy of temptation in this man's life, mixing "15" with "8", and the destructiveness of "8" and "9". On February 19, 2010, Woods gave a televised statement in which he apologized for his

---

[23] "Tiger Woods Biography: Golfer (1975–)".  Biography.com (FYI / A&E Networks).

[24] Woods, Earl, McDaniel, Pete.   (1997).  "Training a Tiger: Raising a Winner in Golf and in Life".

[25] Goldiner, Dave. (December 29, 2012). "Tiger Woods' mistress scandal costs shareholders of sponsors like Nike, Gatorade $12 billion"  NY Daily News.

actions. He said, "I thought I could get away with whatever I wanted to. I felt that I had worked hard my entire life and deserved to enjoy all the temptations around me. I felt I was entitled. Thanks to money and fame, I didn't have to go far to find them. I was wrong. I was foolish."[26]

Aside from the negative influence of some of his number combinations, Tiger Woods had an amazing career. He broke numerous golf records, and won too many awards to list here. Some of those have been the "PGA Player of the Year", a record eleven times,[27] the "Byron Nelson Award", a record eight times, winning 14 professional major golf championships, 18 World Golf Championships, and 79 PGA Tour events. Woods is the youngest player to achieve the career "Grand Slam". He was inducted into the "California Hall of Fame", and been named "Athlete of the Decade". [28] This is only a very partial listing of all his achievements.

Next, lets look at the life of a timeless and well-loved actress, Julia Roberts:

Julia **12/3**  Roberts **25/7**

3 + 7 = **10/1 TNN**

Day of Birth: October **28/1**

Hidden Number: **38 (same as 29)**

---

[26] "Transcript: Tiger's public statement". (February 19, 2010).

Web.tigerwoods.com. ASAP Sports. February 19, 2010.

[27] Kelley, Brent. (October 20, 2009). "Woods Clinches PGA Player of the Year Award". About.com: Golf.

[28] "Tracking Tiger". (June 3, 2009). NBC Sports.

Period Number:  **-9**

Immediately, the first thing I notice in Julia's numbers is her TNN and Day Number, being in harmony under the powerful number "1". The "10" is a number of success, and protects her to a large degree, from the negative qualities of the "28". With the "10" and two "1s", this woman can accomplish just about anything she sets her mind on achieving. I notice that her Hidden Number, although a "38", is in harmony with her Day and TNN as well. Any grief caused by the "38" will be overcome. Julia seems like such a strong person, but the Hidden Number, being an emotional "2", pops up, and we feel the heart and soul of this woman come through, in her ability to bring believable and heart-felt emotion, into any role she plays. She is likable and we relate to her, because we sense she cares, and has been through the pains of experience in life. Its worth noting that the "38" has the same meaning as "29", and although her present marriage, at the time of this writing, seems long-lasting and harmonious, I can not help but think there may be difficulties ahead, or all may not be as it seems.

Julia's first name, although beautiful, is not a positive number. Twelve is the number of sacrifice. It is highly probable that this woman has had to make huge sacrifices to get where she is in her career, or feels her life is at the mercy of it on some level. Her Period Number of "9" helps to harmonize this number, to some degree. As she is usually called "Julia Roberts", and not just "Julia" (like "Angelina") by the media, the influence of the "12" is reduced, and the "10/1" name crowns her. She is known, and succeeds, by her own intentions. The lessons learned through the "12" and the "38", (which is related to the "29"), may be the reason she tends to keep her personal life private, and out of the public eye, as much as possible.

"Roberts" is an excellent number for success, being the lucky "25/7". The "7" also brings good fortune in its harmonious connection with the TNN, Day and Hidden Numbers. This woman has balance in her personal and professional lives. We feel a sense of the authentic with Julia, that what you see is what you get.

(Michael   **22**   King   **11/2**)

Martin   **17/8**   Luther   **25/7**   King   **11/2**   Jr   **3**

**20/2 TNN**

Day of Birth: January **15/6**

Hidden Number: **35/8**

Period Number: **8**

This is a man I greatly admire. He is one of those people who changes us, by his courage and wisdom. To begin with, MLK has a theme of "11" and "4" in his numbers. The year of his birth is 1929, has the last two digits equaling "11", and the total year equals "22/4". His original name, "Michael King", also carries the "11" and "22/4". (If he had used this name, it would have given him a Hidden Number of "12", although he was sacrificed anyway, even with the new numbers, as I'll explain why.) He has an "8" theme, with the "17", "35" and "8", so his life was placed in the hands of fate, as well as guiding and influencing the fate and future of a nation. He was assassinated on April 4th, 1968 (a doubled "4" of the month and day). Holiday celebrations in his honor began in 1971, (a year ending in "8"). His death became a federal holiday in 1986 (a reversal of 1968), and a monument in D.C. was dedicated in

2011 (the year ending in "11" and equaling a "4"). [29]

In observing his personal numbers, the first thing I notice is the three "8s", with a "2" TNN. Secondly, I note that his day of birth is the 15th. This is not a fortunate combination with the "8s". In particular, the "35", carries a heavy warning, and is amplified with the other "8s", and the "15", which brings in dark-side destructive energy. The "17" ensures one's name being remembered after death, as an instrument of peace, but in this case with the fatalistic "8s", and dark side betrayal of the "15", his death will not be a happy one. He was killed for the words that he spoke (his "11" is unsupported), as the eleven can mean getting into trouble for speaking one's mind. It is his very manner of death, and his message, though, that makes us remember him as the great man that he was, and we learn from his words and example of love, peace and brotherhood.

Robin **17** Williams **22**

**12 TNN**

Day of Birth: July **21**

Hidden Number: **33**

Period Number: **2**

Upon hearing of his death today, I wanted to see Robin's numbers, and decided to add him to this book. Robin Williams' destiny numbers contain the lucky "17", "21" and "33". He also has his TNN and Day Number in harmony. The "33" is help from those in higher places. Upon graduating from high school, he was one, of only a small number, chosen to

---

[29] Manheimer, Ann S. (2004). *Martin Luther King Jr.: Dreaming of Equality.* Twenty-First Century Books.

attend Julliard, and one, of only two, accepted into the Advanced Program. Almost immediately after leaving Julliard, he was cast in "The Richard Pryor Show", a "Happy Days" episode, and within two years had his own television sitcom, "Mork and Mindy". He became known for his stand-up comedy, voice-overs, television and Broadway appearances, and many successful movies.[30] He was convincing in any role and setting.

A supported "12", alters the sacrifice required by others that comes with this number, making him a slave to public demand, such as many celebrities. Any sacrifice this individual makes, would be of his own choosing. When we look at his life, it was one of continual success, yet this man was anything but peaceful or happy. He has publicly proclaimed that he abused alcohol and cocaine, to escape depression and loneliness.   Alcohol became his biggest nemesis.[31] It is interesting that just glancing at his astrology chart shows three water placements for his sun, moon and rising sign, with Neptune in the twelfth house, and moon in the fourth. This could be an indicator for an attraction to alcohol. The "17/8" of his first name is a fatalistic number, combined with the "22/4" of the last name, increasing fate's control of this man's life. The "22" is represented by "suffering and anxiety of mind". Robin Williams definitely lived in his mind, and depression was an ongoing battle for him. (It has been shown in tests that negative thoughts are not caused by depression. Depression is

---

[30]  Maslon, Laurence, and Kantor, Michael. *Make 'em Laugh: The Funny Business of America*, Twelve, 2008 pp. 241–244

[31]  Vokes- Dudgeon, Sophie. (August 12, 2014).  Us Magazine.

caused by negative thoughts.) The "22" was leading him to his own downfall with the "12". Robin ended up committing suicide. Additional details of the circumstances of his death have not been released, as of the writing of this book. Although his loss is felt, his name will most definitely live on after him, with the "17/8" promise,  of being remembered with love.

## Tupac and the Recurring 4, 5 and 7

(Born: Lesane   **22**   Parish   **20**   Crooks   **24**)

Tupac   **22/4**   Shakur   **19/1**

2Pac   **14/5**

2Poc   **20/2**

Makaveli   **23**

**TNN: 5, 14, 20, 23**

Day of Birth: June **16**

Hidden Number: **12, 12, 36, 12**

Period Number: **5**

Died:  September **13**, 1996

Tupac Shakur lived a troublesome life, and became known as an actor, and one of the most influential and controversial rappers of all time.[32] At first glance, his life, to me, seemed to be one acted out of anger, crime, vengeance and materialism, until I dug a little deeper. In his numbers, I notice the "22" and the "20", because they are found in his birth name, and are

---

[32] Hindustantimes. (June 16, 2012). *Happy Birthday Tupac!.*

repeated in his stage or public names. Twenty suggests a difficult childhood that shapes the individual's life. I also notice the unsupported "16" and "12". These suggest a fall, and a sacrifice waiting to happen. He has incredible numbers of success, such as the "24", "19", "14", "5" and "36". Tupac seems to have a repeating theme in his life of the numbers "5" and "7", and the number "4" (which can have a fatalistic affect on his "12" and "16"). The lucky "5s" have pushed him to success, and the "14" gave skills as a songwriter and actor (speaking and writing). Note that he also has the "1" and "4" INNs together in his name.

Tupac was shot on a "7" day (September 7) in a "7" year (1996). He died on Friday, September 13th, (a "4" day, and the "death number") at age 25 (adding to "7"). He was pronounced dead at 4:03p.m. (adding to "7"). He was leaving the Death Row owned "Club 662", (adding to 14/5) now known as "Club Seven". He rode in a BMW 750il (BMW adding to "12", "750" adding to "12" and "750il" adding to "16").[33]

Although his other numbers can be seen recurring in all his accomplishments, dates and numbers of records sold, I think it is interesting that "All Eyez on Me" was the fourth studio album by 2Pac featuring five singles. It was released on February 13th by Death Row Records. (It is recognized as one of the crowning achievements of 1990s rap music.) His run-ins with the law and other escapades were on significant dates as well. On August "22" (22/4), he was arrested, at age 22, with a possible 1-4 years in prison, and a 1.4 million bail. (Notice the "1s" and "4s"). He was sentenced on April 5th (a "4" month "5"

[33] Planas, Antonio. (April 7, 2011). *FBI Outlines Parallels in Notorious B.I.G., Tupac Slayings.* Las Vegas Review-Journal.

day). In 1994 (a "5" year) he was shot *five* times. He began serving a prison sentence on Feb. 14(14/5). Got married on April 4 1996 (a "4" month, "4" day). His album "The Don Killuminati: The 7 Day Theory", was named after the *seven* days it took to write, record and produce it. He changed his name to Makaveli, which was a fortunate number "23/5", but again produced the "12" Hidden Number of sacrifice.[34]

Even though Tupac's lyrics were graphic, vengeful, violent and disturbing (reflecting the struggles of black youth), his actual message was very different when he spoke publicly or was interviewed. He believed in God, racial equality, and making this a better country. He wanted to uplift the black youth. I find it interesting that he was never convicted or found fully guilty of any of his "crimes".

---

[34] McQuillar, Tayannah Lee. Johnson, Fred L. PhD. (January 26, 2010). *Tupac Shakur: The Life and Times of an American Icon.*

# CHAPTER NINE

# First, Middle and Last Names

Since most people don't usually go by their full name in casual settings, your first name is likely the name most often spoken, when people address you. As its influence is increased by its use, the number representing the total of the first name (INN) then, can be considered pretty important. It is wise, to consider making sure that this number is a fortunate one.

Something interesting to think about, is that people with the same first name, would share the same name (INN) number. If the name "John" equals "18/9" (1 + 7 + 5 + 5), you could say that all people named John are sharing the influence of the "18/9", and so would have things in common, between them. If you altered the spelling of the name "John" to "Jon", you would have a different energy, because "Jon" would be "1 + 7 + 5 = 13/4". Dropping the "h" gives these two names different INN name numbers, of "18" and "13".

Note that if you did not see the names written, you would not be aware of the difference in spelling, because both of these names are pronounced the same. The phonetics of their names, (how they sound), can give them a similarity. Identical sound frequencies could share similar characteristics from their phonetics alone. So in this form of Chaldean Numerology, you could say that you are calculating the energies of written words. This involves eyesight. If we were to work with phonetics, which requires the sense of hearing, we could decode these energies as well. This relates to a branch of Chaldean connected to the Hebrew Alphabet, and its interpretations of the sounds of vowels, and combinations of consonants. For example, the letter "A" can have a long sound, as in "aim", or a short sound as in "apple", or *aw* in "law". Depending on the vowel phonetic, a number value would be assigned to the letter "A". If it is a long "A", it would be assigned the number "2". The short "A's" would be assigned the number value "1". There are also differences in the consonant letters, such as "T" or "S", when they are alone or combined with an "H". Phonetic numerology will not be covered in this book, as it has different rules from this one presented. I leave it to you, the reader, to explore and expand your own studies.

In addition to names sharing the same INNs, and phonetics, you also give characteristics to names, based on your experiences with them. So if you have had a liking for people named "John", your opinion of the name "John" adds to the collective unconscious, defining the energy of that name, and its future use.

# The First Name as an Archetype

As you individually add energy to names by your experiences with other people, you help define name characteristics in the overall mass consciousness. Sigmund Freud, the father of psychoanalysis, has surmised that we live out our adult lives through the filters set by individual childhood traumas buried in our unconscious. Meaning, if someone was bullied in childhood, they will continue to play the victim of bullies in various circumstances throughout adulthood. On the other hand, Carl Jung, a Swiss psychiatrist, had come to a different conclusion, about the unconscious mind and its influence. He believed that we were a combined collective pool of consciousness, and that this mass pool found outlets through each individual's unconscious mind to express itself. In other words, when we played the victim role in adulthood, we were not channeling our own buried experience of being bullied as a child, but rather *everyone's* experience of being bullied. Bullying and victimization are archetypes in the overall unconscious. So, whether someone was beat up by kids at school, controlled by their older sister, threatened by a parent and so on, it made no difference, as it was all "bullying". Bullying in the collective consciousness will find a way to channel itself into everyone's life in some way. So, the adult acting out a victim role, in adult life, is channeling *everyone's experience* who had ever been bullied, not just their own.

In this same way, when we take on a first name, we channel from the collective unconscious, the energy of everyone who ever had that name. All "Janes" are tapped into the archetype "Jane", so to speak. Names take on a mythology, just as there are 12 signs in the Zodiac, that follow archetypal traits. Is it not interesting, then, that names can subtly or unconsciously allude to someone's character, without knowing anything about the person? It is as if hearing a name tells us something about someone, or causes a reaction of like, dislike or indifference in us. Sometimes this can be attributed to knowing someone from the past with that particular name, and sometimes it has no explanation.

I was speaking with one of my friends (I'll call her Julie), about some events that had occurred surrounding a particular woman. Before I could get to the part of how this woman had made me suffer, Julie asked me what the woman's name was. When I told her "Tamara" (names are changed here), she said, "Oh, she sounds like a mean person." It made me wonder if Julie had had negative experiences with someone named "Tamara", as she based most of her opinion on this woman's name alone. Did her experience with "Tamara" come about through personal experience, or was she tapping into the unconscious mass pool of thought? I asked Julie if she had known a Tamara before, and she said, "No."

I have a client who does not like anyone named Cathy. She was okay with women named Kathy with a "K", but not with the "C". When I asked her the reason for this, she did not really know. She just said "Cathys" always seem to turn out as she expects them to: "whiny" and, according to her, "irritating", whereas the "Kathys" were much more likable. (No offense meant here, as I happen to love "Cathys"!) I think to some degree we all have preconceived notions or prejudices about certain names, possibly from a shared unconscious past life memory.

As times and fashions change, a name can become undesirable. For example, the name "Gertrude", in its day probably implied an attractive woman. In my generation, a person might initially laugh if you said your name was "Gertrude", or not believe you. (I don't mean offense to any Gertrudes, but it is not a name I have ever known anyone to have, and not commonly used today. I don't know why the name is funny, or why it implies an elderly outdated person in my culture. I am sure there are some wonderful Gertrudes, and if I met one, my impression of the name would probably change.) We all do this. We cannot help it, as we are, according to Jung, vehicles for the connected unconscious mind.

In summary, then, first names tend to take on the persona of all the people who have owned the name. As you live out your life under a certain name, your experiences add to the name's perception in the future collective mind. Therefore, names and our perception of them change, like the Gertrude example above. They have an energy and life of their own, through the influence of those who have held and lived the name, other's opinion of them, and the numbers that make up the name. In a sense, the name becomes its own archetype.

## Your Family Name

Your last name is shared with those in your family, and represents your connection to your ancestry. The use of this name can bring with it, all the blessings, curses, karma, associations and ancestral history of that side of the family. With the name, you take on everything that goes and has gone with it. Its as if you are merged with the energy, and carrying it forward. What is your family history? What has seemed to be a common theme, with relatives sharing your last name? Do you need to do some healing, or break ties with some negative family patterns? These are questions you may want to ask yourself, before using this name in the future. Sometimes a shaman or healer can help with deep-seated ancestral issues, as well as working through present family karma, with psychoanalysis and forgiveness.

Unless someone is actually called by their last name, this is usually a name only spoken formally, in introductions, or written on legal documents. Therefore, I do not see a lot of connection between families who share a common last name, such as Smith or Jones. The connections happen on a personal level, with one's own family and personal history. If, however, you are often called by your last name, or it is used a lot in connection with you, then its number would be very prominent in your life.

In the case of an unfortunate last name INN, one should consider changing the name in some way. Sometimes it can seem difficult to change your last name, because others, such as family members or a spouse, may feel offended. Grandpa may be expecting you to carry on the family name, or as a woman, your husband may be insulted if you don't want to take his name. Family can get sensitive, so if you absolutely must keep an unfortunate last name, to keep the peace and avoid offending anyone, then be absolutely certain, that all of your other numbers are fortunate. A second option is to use a different last name in your business, social media or career, and use your birth name in private matters. Remember, if you decide to keep a negative number last name, even part of the time, it will still affect your life.

When changing the name, a married woman can try using her maiden name, if her married name is not giving her a fortunate number. Another way to alter the last name is adding or deleting a letter or two, such as one "L" instead of two, or doubling a letter. An example would be "Watson" or "Wattson". In some cases a completely new last name is needed.

*My view is that a woman's last name is just as important as a man's. Consider this: There is never a doubt about a child's maternity, as there is with paternity, so wouldn't it be wiser for the norm to be, that children and husbands take on the mother's last name?*

## Middle Names

For most people, the middle name is only used, when signing a legal document that asks for the middle name or initial. In numerology, it can be very useful, when changing one's name. In some circumstances, the middle name can be substituted for a first name, which has an unfortunate INN number. One could also use the middle initial to influence or change one's name numbers. In the name "Billie Mason", one could change the first name spelling, and use "Billy Mason" instead. Another option would be adding the middle initial, "Billie J. Mason". If this person uses the middle name and is known as "Billy Joe", they could drop the name "Joe" or "Billy" to create more harmonious numbers.

## Baby Names

Picking a name for your baby is important, because in that name lies the luck and success of their future experiences. Since one cannot control the day the child is born, (outside of induced labors), it would be best to wait until after the child is born, to make sure the name will be harmonious to the Day Number, and creates a positive Hidden Number. You would do the same number chart, and follow the same rules as you would for an adult. Also consider the town you reside in and its harmony with your child's name and birth date.

CHAPTER TEN

# Synchronicities and Numbers

When asked, "What is your favorite number?", many of us have a digit that comes to mind that we like, or may consider our "lucky number". Usually this is a number that shows up repetitively in our lives, or a number that has a positive experience connected to it, such as winning contests or lotteries, or your child being born on a certain day, etc. The energies of numbers do affect us, and certain ones do seem to be attracted to us.

# Recurring Numbers

In your personal life, certain numbers may be predominant, continuing to show up everywhere in addresses, license plates, receipt totals, bank account numbers or ID numbers and the like. Or maybe you were born on the 3rd, are the 3rd son, your parents were married on the 3rd, you have three children, events happen to you in 3 year cycles and so on. It is very common for numbers to recur in an individual's life, marking important events and milestones. Are you noticing unusual synchronicities with numbers? It is important to notice these coincidental sequences, as it may show you what number is dominating your life.

If your Day Number is a "4" or "8", it can be especially helpful to be aware if one or both are recurring, or are attracted to you in life. Are they bringing negative or positive experiences? If the "4" or "8" are popping up everywhere, notice what occurred on those dates, events, circumstances or with the people who have these numbers. If troublesome, it would be wise to use one of the strong numbers of "1", "3", "5" or "6" to replace the harmful "4" or "8" influence in your life.

## Numbers in Families

You may notice a particular number that seems to repeat in your family. This can be a number being passed from generation to generation, such as your grandfather always having coincidences with the number "13", that passes down to your father and you. There could be a history of repetitious patterns with the family name number, as well.

This family has a last name INN of "20/2", which created a

"2" recurring theme. The effects of the "20" are also carried forward, with those who kept the last name, and those who did not:

# Family Theme of "2"

(There are 7 children in the family)

- The letters in the family's last name add to "20", which reduces to a "2".
- The father's full name adds to 2.
- The mother's first name adds to 2.
- Three children are born on the 2nd of the month.
- 2 children are born on "1" days.
- 2 family members are born on "4" days, and they are the only 2 astrology fire signs.
- This leaves 2 members left with unmatched birth dates.
- There are 2 boys, and they are the only 2 children born on unmatched dates.
- The first child was male born in the 2nd month.
- He was 2nd to 2 miscarriages.
- His first name adds to 22, and his nickname is a 2.
- The 2nd child is female, born on the 2nd of March.
- The total of her birth date adds to 2.
- She married and now her name adds to 2.
- She has 2 children.
- There are 4 children, whose full name adds to 2.
- 2 are born on the 28th.
- 2 are born during the 11th month, which is a 2 month.
- Every family member is born on an even day, a multiple of 2.
- All grandchildren are multiples of 2. (One grandchild was

lost, making now 4 children in that family, although never forgotten.)
- 2 of the children are gay, and chose not to have grandchildren.
- The 2 remaining unmarried children did not have children, despite efforts to do so.

## My Parents & the Numbers "4" and "8"

My parents are born on "4" and "8" days. People with the personal numbers of "4's" and "8's" can have very fate-directed lives, and repeatedly attract these numbers to themselves. Here are just a few of their major milestones:
- My dad is born on the 26th, an 8 day.
- He is born during the 8th month.
- His birth year 1926, ends with 2 and 6, adding to an 8.
- My dad's last birthday before he died was 8-26-2006. (An 8 day, 8 month, 8 year - as 2006 adds to 8).
- My Mom is born on the 4th.
- She is born in the 4th month.
- The "31" of her birth year 1931 adds to 4.
- My mother's Total Name Number adds to 4.
- My mother's Hidden Number is a 4.
- The total of her birthdate is 4.
- The letters of my mother's maiden name add to 8.
- They celebrated their last anniversary together in 2006 which adds to 8.
- The entire anniversary date adds to 17/8.
- Their phone number 447-5627, added to 8.
- My Dad died in his 80th year.

## My Parents Marriage & the 3-6-9 Series

My parents were married on a "3" day, which triggered the series of 3-6-9 repeating, and at times taking over the energy of the "4" and "8". This is a sampling of this 3-6-9 theme (see Chapter 7 on "Numbers and Compatibility").

- My parents were married on the 30th, a 3 day.
- They were married in the 6th month.
- The year of marriage 1956 adds to 21, a 3.
- The total date of their marriage adds to 30/3.
- The address of their house was 3117, adding to a 12/3.
- My dad died on June 24th, a 6 day in the 6th month.
- The year my dad died, 2007 adds to 9.
- Adding up the entire date of his death adds to 21/3.
- There were 9 family members.
- The office building he owned and worked in, added to a 6.
- 4 children were born relating to a 3-6-9 series date - 24th, 3rd month, 6th month, 9th month. That leaves 3 born on 2 dates.
- Their first-born was the 3rd pregnancy, after two miscarriages, and was born on the 24th, a 6 day. He worked in the 6 office with my father.

## The "4" and "8" in the Presley Family

- Vernon Presley was the illegal age of 17, when he married Gladys (17 adds to 8).
- Vernon and Gladys Presley were married on the 17th of June, an "8" day.
- At the end of June 1934, Gladys knew she was pregnant. That year adds to 17, an "8". Elvis was born on Jan. 8, 1935, an "8" day. His twin brother was stillborn,

symbolizing the "8s" connection to sorrow with the "2". Gladys lost her mother that year in 1935, the last two digits totally "8".

- Vernon receives a check for only $4 for the sale of a hog. He felt cheated, and he and his brother were accused of altering the amount to $40. Both "4s". On January 4th 1938, a "4" day, Vernon does not receive a bond for bail from his father. Vernon ends up being sentenced to prison. He was released in 1939 - adding to a "22/4".

- When Elvis was 13 (a "4"), his family packed up and left for Memphis in 1948, a year which adds to "22/4".

- The family bought a home in Memphis, with the address 1034 Audubon Drive, the number adding to an "8".

- On March 17 1957 - an "8" day in a "4" year, Elvis buys Graceland.

- Elvis loses his mother at age 22 - equaling a "4". [35]

- Elvis' last concert was in Indianapolis, on June 26, 1977, an "8" day.

- They considered Jesse Garon the fourth member of the family.

- Vernon divorces his second wife after 17 years, an "8".

- Vernon, the last member of their family, dies on the 26th of June, 1979, an "8" day with the entire year adding to a "4".

As I have shown in an earlier example, Elvis and his twin Jesse shared number similarities in their names. Their birthdate is an "8". "Elvis Presley" equals "18". "Jesse" is a "17". "Garon" is an "18". Jesse's TNN is "17". Elvis' Hidden Number

---

[35] Australia, Elvis. (January 24, 2010). *Vernon and Gladys Presley : Elvis Presley's Mother and Father.*

is "17". Jesse's Hidden Number is "16" (the Falling Tower, or Shattered Citadel). Their Period Number is an "8".

In addition to the "4s" and "8s", the father, Vernon Presley has a connection to the number "16". Here are a few of the recurrences: He was born in 1916, the year ending in "16". He was kicked out of the house at age 16. His only son died on August 16[th.] The year he married Gladys was 1933, adding to 16. On Nov. 16th he was indicted for the forgery of the $4 check altercation. His second wife Dee, divorced her husband in 1960, adding to a 16, to marry Vernon. He died in 1979, the last two digits adding to a 16. The second wife, whom he divorced, and seemed to be a source of anguish for Elvis, died at age 88, adding to a 16. [36]

# 11:11, 33 & Other Mysterious Numbers

You may have heard of the "11:11" phenomenon, which started in the early 90s, where large numbers of people have been noticing 11:11 everywhere they look. In addition to the 11:11, many people are frequently seeing other number patterns, such as "1234", "11:33", "12:12" or "1333", and so on. There is a lot of speculation, as to what these coincidental number sequences mean.

It is believed that the "11:11", "1:11" or "11", is considered a doorway to a higher vibration of evolution, as the Earth moves into this more enlightened frequency. Synchronicities are related to this shift. I see the 11:11 as two doorways, representing the "battle" between light and dark, or good and bad. I feel that these energy doorways have opened up, and people are being given a choice which door they are going to

---

[36] Carrell, Sharon. *Vernon*. Tripod.com

take. Are you going to side with the light, and choose to allow your soul to evolve spiritually, or are you going to get sucked into the dark side, and remain stuck in the false power and suffering of an illusory world? These doorways can also be likened to choosing God Self or the ego. (Some are of the belief that this evolvement opportunity will take us into a 5th dimensional reality.) There is a major fight, or last ditch effort happening right now, by those that would see us held back, to keep people in the darkness of ignorance, pain, anger, grief and suffering. A fight for souls, or the age-old battle between the light and the dark. It may be a time to make your choice. I also view the 11:11 as a doorway, for many souls to enter and exit, during this time of accelerated evolution. The 11:11, for me, is also a revolving doorway, meaning that cycles come and go. We evolve, then devolve, in an endless loop. Some see 11:11 as a divine alignment timing, for Twin Flames to reunite.

A lot of these noticeable number repetitions and combinations relate to the sacred geometry of the universe. These numbers are markers along the way, of synchronous happenings and alignments. It is also thought that we are in a type of matrix computer program, similar to the ideas in the movie, "The Matrix". Number repetitions and serendipities are information about where we are in the matrix hologram. It is the very confinement of this program, that makes the choice for evolution, as mentioned above, necessary.

In a nutshell, realize that the energies of such numbers as "33", "13" etc., represent the light side, and have positive messages, but are also being used by the dark side to trap, enslave and ensnare. Your intention and choice to evolve, or not to evolve will decide their influence on you, good or ill. This is a world of duality. While 11:11 has many positive connotations in the "New Age" movement, if you are a realist, you will have to consider the other side of things as well.

## Lincoln and Kennedy, or Kennedy and Lincoln, or Lincoln...

A common comparison between the synchronicities of Abraham Lincoln and John F. Kennedy's lives has been going around the internet, on multiple sites. How much of it is true, I am uncertain, but it is an interesting read, as ""Lincoln" and "Kennedy" both add to "27". Here is an interesting link, with similarities in their appearance:

www.neardeath.com/experiences/reincarnation08.html

# CHAPTER ELEVEN

# A Brief Introduction to Timing & Prediction

suggest that this section be approached, after you have a full grasp of the personal numbers and their rules, as addressed in previous chapters. Going too quickly into this learning can be overwhelming, and discourage you from what is actually an easy system to learn, if you remember the rules of it.

So far, you have studied the numbers, and what type of experiences they are suggesting, but not *when* these circumstances are likely to occur. In this chapter, I want to introduce you to ways of predicting the timing of events, as well as what triggers them. Always remember, that if you are willing to change unfortunate personal numbers, disturbing or tragic events can be avoided, or decreased in severity. Lucky numbers will help bypass, what could have been a cause for suffering.

# The Triggers

First, *it is important to become familiar with any recurring numbers or number themes in your life* (as discussed in the previous chapter). This will help determine what number(s) is directing your life, which may provide clues pointing to the possible timing of events. I call these "triggers", as they seem to ignite or set the stage for playing out the circumstances of your personal destiny numbers, and their predictive meanings (found in Chapter Two). Some of the main triggers are: locations, the Pattern of Destiny, the birth year, the current year, the numbers "4" and "8" and the person's age numbers. I will discuss each of these here separately. A knowledge of Astrology and Palmistry prediction is also helpful, for confirmations of what the numbers may show.

## Location Trigger

When an individual decides to move to a new location, the city/town and number address of the house can trigger one of their personal destiny numbers to play out, whether this be fortunate or unfortunate. A location trigger does not include the street name, as there is more than one lot/residence on a given street. The address number, that identifies the house, apartment or structure where the individual resides, is considered the location, as well as considering the city number, which gives an overall contributing influence of the entire area's energy. The county is more of a general influencer, as there are multiple cities/towns in a county. The same is true for the state (or whatever is similar in your country). Out of these, the address number will have the most influence on an individual's personal life. (Pay attention to the addresses of businesses, work or other important places, as well as your home.)

Here is a heartbreaking story of a strong "1" person attracting sorrow, disaster and possible death, through the number "4" (I have not used actual names for the sake of privacy). You can easily observe the combination of the location and 4-8(see next section) triggers. I share this story in hopes that their loss was not in vain, and others can help themselves by learning about destiny numbers.

*Wife:*
"First Name" = **8**   "Last Name" = **40/4**

TNN = **12/3**

Day Number: **28/1**

Hidden Number: **40/4**

Period Number: **2**

*Husband:*
"First Name" = **9**   "Last Name" = **40/4**

TNN = **13/4**

Day Number: **13/4**

Hidden Number: **26/8**

Period Number: **8**

City of Residence: **22/4**

Right away, you can see a 4-8 number theme. She has an Unsupported TNN Number of "12", which does not harmonize with the Day Number "28/1". Being unsupported, the sacrificial nature of the "12" is going to play itself out in this woman's life, especially since the Period Number is a "2", which is at the mercy of the "8" in the first name. (See rules for #2). Adding to the "8" influence, is the repeated "40/4" in both the last name and her Hidden Number, an unfortunate number that also increases the "8" energy. (Remember that the number "4" can sometimes spell pain, hardship and loss for "one" people.) Since "4"s and "8"s are the numbers of fate (see rules for number "4" and "8"), we see that the twelve sacrifice is going to be beyond her control.

This woman got pregnant, in her 13<sup>th</sup> year of marriage, also a "4", and the "death/renewal" number. A few months before her delivery, the couple decides to move their family to a new home. The address of this home is "813", showing the energies of this house. Even the line-up of those three numbers, an "8" with a "13", is disturbing, considering their connection to this couple's numbers. You will also notice that the address adds to a "12", so the "12" just got doubled as a warning (the "12/3" is unsupported, as well). The couple moves in, has their 4<sup>th</sup> child, and "3" months later, lose the baby. This woman, a good mother and well-versed in the medical field, could do nothing to prepare for this, prevent it or save her baby. It was out of her hands. In looking at the warnings or predictions for the timing of this event, "moving to a new address" was obviously the trigger.

The first thing I notice about her husband's numbers, is all the "4s" (which were created in his wife's numbers, by taking his last name, making her Hidden Number "40", as well). When fours are multiplied, they create "8" energy. Looking at their numbers together, they have three "8s" and two thirteens. When they moved, the address triggered the change in vibration of their path. The husband has the "13" energy of the "813" address. The negative side of the "13" is playing out as death, when combined with the unsupported "12", and the "8"s and "4"s. They were living in a ""22/4" city. Had this couple moved to the adjacent city of the mother's birth, the same may have happened, as that city's vibration is twelve. With the "8" and "13" together in the address, and in their personal numbers, the "8" was also a 4-8 trigger (see next section) of the "13".

Two years after the loss of their infant, the couple was able to have another child, who helped heal their wounds enough that the family could go on. This is the literal renewal/rebirth of the "13". They now have four children (here is the "4" again - with the fifth never forgotten). Fours and eights may be lucky for this couple, but the problems in their numbers needed to be fixed, so the 4 and 8 would not have helped trigger the negative numbers.

Had I known what I do now, about numerology, I'm not sure that I could have warned this couple or what could have been done different. Since this information was not available at that time, this was something they were pre-destined to go through in this lifetime, and part of the baby's destiny in the over-all divine plan (which we cannot always see or know from our small perspective).

## The 4-8 Trigger

The 4-8 trigger is often found combined with the other triggers, as in the previous example. The number "8" can trigger events, and activate other numbers. If the individual has personal numbers that are not harmonious with an eight, or other problems in their numbers, these events will be unfortunate in nature. If the eight has been shown to bring good karma to the individual's life, then the events triggered can be fortunate. An eight can enter, and act as a precursor or sign of this fate when showing up in addresses, other people, partners, membership numbers, dates, age, etc.

An "8" will trigger the negative qualities of a "12", "13", "15", "16", "18" and any of the remaining unfortunate numbers, especially if these numbers are unsupported. It can also trigger events in the life of a "2", "4", "7", "8" or "9" person. (An example of the eight triggering an event is found in Steve Job's Pattern of Destiny from Chapter Seven.)

A number "4" will trigger events, if there are other "4s", "8s" or "9s" involved, or in the case of a "1" individual, who has noticed the "4" bringing hardship and loss.

## The Birth Year Trigger

It is common for the last two digits of an individual's birth year to be a determining factor in recurring themes. For example, someone born in 1967 would add the "67", which has the value of "13". The sixty-seven and thirteen can become significant numbers in life, signaling important changes, events and good fortune when they pop up. The first two digits of the birth year are not used in this fashion (which in this case would be "19"), as they represent an entire century, and several generations of people. The total of the year is used in calculating the Pattern of Destiny, but this number could also signify a lucky or significant number for the individual, as well. In this case, if you add "1967", it would be "23". If one of these birth year numbers recurs in their life (the 67, 13 or 23), look for it as a trigger of events. The nature of these events will be determined by the nature of the numbers themselves (whether boding ill-luck or good fortune).

## The Current Year Trigger

As I write this chapter, the year is 2015. The current year number predicts an energy trend for that year. *Current years affect us in two ways: the total number of the year, and the last two digits of the year.* This year, 2015, adds to "8". The last two digits are "15". The rules of numbers say, that a "15" combined with "4s" and "8s", brings in sinister and deceptive agendas and energies. In 2015 we are in an "8" year with a "15".

I have noticed that the "4" and "8" days this year, seem to bring misfortune, taking on a dark side energy (associated with abuse, addiction, demonic forces, manipulation and material loss). This type of energy can bring up feelings of fear and a loss of control. This does not mean we have to be slaves to this energy. It is important to note that individuals who were born with karmic reward, from the numbers "4" and "8", may look at this year as a boon, finding much worldly and financial success, and the reaching of their goals.

As I write this, the most recent 4-8 day was March 8, followed by Friday the 13th. On the eighth, Sam Simon (co-creator of "The Simpsons") died, a close relative of mine was on week four, of a six week recovery, and had to go back into emergency surgery for relapse (this has led to a loss of livelihood and body function), my boyfriend had a large amount of money taken from him by a deceptive person (money he badly needed), and I had my own share of bad luck. Only five days later, on the 13th, I had many unfortunate issues come up for me again, our dog had to go to the vet with a serious condition, and a friend's mother died. I tried to stay home that day and avoid the world, but it did not help. Being a "2", I am inclined to stay home on all "4" and "8" days this year, especially during the "4" and "8" months of April and August! (Note: Sam Simon has an "8" INN, a "20" Inn, and "16" as an unsupported Hidden Number.)

Other days that may affect us negatively, during this "8" year, would be "2" days. Remember in rules of numbers, that 8s may bring monetary reward or assistance to a "2", but there is pain, loss and suffering that come with it. The "8" dominates the "2", and therefore makes "2" days under this type of energy under the control of something else. On March 20, I was issued a bizarre notice from my apartment complex that I owed back rent since February 1, and I was being charged $5/day since then. My cable and internet would be immediately shut off, if I did not pay within the next half hour before the office closed for the day. When I got to the apartment office, there was a line of tenants who had received similar notices, many of whom said they were being evicted immediately. Apparently my past due amount was $6, which had somehow increased to $167. No one understood what was going on, and the office assistant was at a loss to explain. We were told to gather all our rent receipts and show up the next day, to disprove the charges. The next day (the 21st), the office manager could not explain the charges, or understand their books. I was told I did not owe anything, and actually received a $107 credit back. I still have no idea what happened. It is worth noting that some "2s" may have a positive experience on "2" days, especially those with several twos in their personal numbers.

A secondary influence to keep in mind in an "8" year, would be "7s" and "9s", as these two numbers do not harmonize with "8s". Also note that the 4th and 17th may have a softer energy than the other 4-8 days, due to these numbers having a more positive vibration than the other dates.

It would be wise to do as little as possible on the "4" and "8" days in 2015, especially if you are a "2", "7", "9", or a "4" or "8" that has negative karmic debt (from "4s" and "8s"). If you noticed these days, and particularly the months of April and August bringing in challenging dark energy, hopefully you just flowed with it. If you stayed in the moment and had an attitude that things would work out, you gave them an opportunity to turn around. This will help with the feeling of having lost control. If you do not react emotionally to an unfortunate circumstance, but rather wait patiently and expect the good, the situation will most of the time change for the better, sometimes right before your eyes. If it is a particularly difficult occurrence, give yourself time to heal, and then open to the possibility of the lesson, gift, message or blessing that accompanied the pain. I am anticipating this year, 2015 will definitely be one of growth.

Here are just a few more examples I am noticing, of this "8" year's influence. As I said, I am a "2" Day Number, my age equals a "2", and I currently use two names. (In the old name, I still have the energy of the unsupported Hidden Number "12", and live in a "12" city.) On April 4, ("8" year, "4" month, "4" day) my boyfriend came back from a Florida trip a changed man. I determined he had picked up dark entities, which turned out to be true. His personality was very different. On April 12 (8 days later), he told me he was moving out (on a "12" day). No warning. Within forty-five minutes he was already out the door. On July 4, I walked into the edge of a door and ended up with a black eye and a gash on my forehead, along with a few other challenges. My elderly mother was sick, and my brother and another person became sick at our July 4th party (7 month, 4 day). On July 8, A friend of mine's (a "2" person) bank account numbers, and other pertinent information got into the wrong hands. An hour later, I could not find my wallet and credit cards. (Note: my boyfriend and I are back together, and stronger than ever. We do not choose to be married, so he remains "boyfriend".)

The last time a year ended in "15" energy, (but without the "8" energy) was 1996. I married a man with a hidden number "13", and an "8" Period Number. These both triggered the last two digits of 1996 (having the same karma as "15"). He was addicted to drugs, but I was too naive to see what was going on. In addition, the day before my wedding, my former boyfriend (who I regretted leaving) killed himself on a "4" day - the 31st - at age 40.He was a Day Number 2. After my divorce, I was left with my ex-husband's debt, which took me eight years of lean living to finally pay off. This is a small sampling of the energies of addiction, loss of control, financial loss and despair, that are tied with the energies of "4s" and "8s" with a "15".

# The Age Number & Pattern of Destiny Triggers

Not only do the numbers of the day or year affect us, so do the numbers of our age. There are two ways our age can be a trigger. The first is the number of the age, such as 5 years old, or 36 years old. The second is the total of our age, such as age "29" added together is "11" and "2". Another contributor to signs of an event occurrence can be found in the Pattern of Destiny trigger. Following are a few examples that include the recurring number themes for these individuals, and how the age number or Pattern of Destiny was the trigger.

Sally is born in a "4" month on a "4" day; the last two digits of her birth year are "31"; she married an "8" husband; her total birth date adds to "4" and her name and Hidden Number are both "4". Immediately we see the recurring number of "4", attracting "8s". Her husband's numbers are mostly "8s" and "9s". This couple chose to be married on a "3" day, setting up the marriage under a 3-6-9 series energy. Important days, addresses etc. followed this series. This was beneficial for the "8" husband, helping release of a lot of the "8s" cruel influence, as this number was one of karmic debt for him. Sally's husband died on a 3-6-9 themed month, day and year. Now that she is a widow, her recurring numbers seem to be in her own series again. Sally's current age is 83. It is possible that she could pass away, when the two numbers 8 and 4 come together, at age 84 this year (being that 2015 is an "8" year ending in "15", which is unlucky when found with "4s" and "8s"). The total of her age, 84, would be "12", the sacrifice number. This is probably unlikely, though, since she no longer has an "8" number connected to her. She could go at age 85, since that age adds to "13" (and her address adds to 16, which would also be the year 2016. This would double that number).

Another age related trigger would be 87, adding to "15". Her other possibility is at age 88, in the year 2020, which would be connected to the Pattern of Destiny Trigger. I do not want to specifically speculate here, as that would involve an analysis of all her destiny numbers together. Sometimes it is better if this is not known.

Sally just had a "4" period followed by an "8" period, in her Pattern of Destiny (see Chapter 7), and is currently in a "7" period ending in 2021. These could have been a signal of fate, of her final pattern period. Otherwise, if she survives this, she will be 89 years old.

My next example is a woman born under the 2-7 influence of recurring numbers. She has three "2s" in her personal numbers. (The rules for number two state that having three numbers in the two series, in your personal numbers, brings general good fortune, and very likely great luck at some point in life, depending on the other numbers. Four or more numbers in the "2" series - two of these being the Day and TNN - brings in great luck at some point in life. Four or more "2s" - four of these being the TNN, Day, Period and Hidden number - suggests a life of great fortune, without major hardships, and will cancel out the energy of unfortunate numbers.) The last two numbers of her year of birth add to "7". She received an unexpected and large windfall of money at the age of 52, in a "2" month, "7" day, in a "7" year.

My next example is a man who had an "8" and "9" recurring influence in his life, (birth year, month, day etc.) which attracted in "4s", "3s" and "6s". He died at age 80 in a "6" month, "6" day, "9" year, with the entire birthdate adding to "3". His Pattern of Destiny shows a repeating "18", up until 1998, when his number changes to a "27" (another "9"). This period will last until 2025. He died exactly 9 years after 1998, in 2007.

He did not make it through this final period of numbers, which was indicated by the change to "27".

For the simplicity of this book, I have discussed this as an introduction. There are other methods of prediction and timing, but discussing this and other methods, in more depth in this work, would prove overwhelming for the beginner, so I leave it to you to further advance your studies and knowledge in this area, at this time.

# Final Thoughts

Whether you are a beginner or a professional numerologist, this book has attempted to show you how to use Chaldean Numerology, to improve your life, your destiny and your experience. I urge you to study several different number systems, and learn the best uses of each. Study the connections of numerology to astrology, palmistry and tarot. If your goal is to improve your luck financially or socially, create stronger relationships and the like, this can be done, but is not at the heart of numbers, nor is it their only purpose. It is your choice. My intent was to stir your passion to delve deeper, into the mysteries of numbers, as a support to our spiritual evolution. I hope your study brings you closer to a state of ecstatic oneness and joy.

Here are some final thoughts to contemplate:

Numbers are used to create time, but the origin of numbers is not measurable or known. In their essence, numbers measure our separation from each other - the separateness in our atomic structure, the space in between you and me, the distance between you and an object etc. In a world of illusions, where perception of separation *creates* the illusion, numbers join us and show us, underneath it all, we are connected, and we are all one. So, numbers seem to measure the separation, but in essence really join us together. The use of numbers is an esoteric mystery, and when studied as "separateness", become "magic" and illusion, but when studied as oneness, bring us back to our one Creator and true reality. We can say, for example that the planet Mars vibrates to the number "9", but this number comes from a deeper cosmological source. It is the beginning and the ending. It is the number of completion. In mystical truths, it leads back to the whole, to oneness, to the Source, which is outside of measurement in this "reality". The number "9" serves as a tool for dissolving illusions as no longer necessary, and ultimately, to the dissolution of the need for numbers. Many blessings to you on your journey!

FOR MORE INFORMATION: Go to my websites:
www.anmarieuber.com
www.5numbersofdestiny.com

# Bibliography

Aristotle. (340 BC). *Teachings.* Stagira: Self Published.

ASAP Sports. (February 19, 2010). *Transcript: Tiger's public statement.* Tigerwoods.com.

Biography.com (FYI / A&E Networks). *"Tiger Woods Biography: Golfer (1975–)".*

Brewer-Giorgio, Gail. *Is Elvis Alive?.*

Brownlee, John. *"37 Years Ago Today, Steve Jobs & Steve Wozniak Invented Apple".*

Carrell, Sharon. *Vernon.* Tripod.com

Carroll, Rober Todd. (1994). *Morphic Resonance.* The Skeptic's Dictionary.

Cheiro's *Book of Numbers.*

Cheiro;s *You and Your Star.*

Elvis Australia. (January 24, 2010). *Vernon and Gladys Presley : Elvis Presley's Mother and Father.*

Ewalt, David M. (October 5, 2011). *Steve Jobs ' 2005 Stanford Commencement Address.* Forbes.

Fontenot, Robert. Elvis Presley Timeline: 1971.

Ganino.com. (April, 1964). *The Chaldean Legend.* THEOSOPHY, Vol. 52, No. 6, (Pages 175-182; Size: 22K)

Geller, Larry. *If I Can Dream.*

Goldiner, Dave. (December 29, 2012). *Tiger Woods' mistress scandal costs shareholders of sponsors like Nike, Gatorade $12 billion.* NY Daily News.

Goodman, Linda. *Star Signs.*

Green, Mary (December 27, 2006). *"Brad and Angelina's New Year's Resolution: Help Cambodia".*People.

Hindustantimes. (June 16, 2012). *Happy Birthday Tupac!.*

Jewish Encyclopedia 1901-1905

Johnson,Ted. *Pitt takes a stand against Prop 8.* Variety.

Kelley, Brent. (October 20, 2009). *Woods Clinches PGA Player of the Year Award*. About.com: Golf.

Lacker, Marty. *"Elvis and the Memphis Mafia".*

Manheimer, Ann S. (2004). *Martin Luther King Jr.: Dreaming of Equality.* Twenty-First Century Books.

Maslon, Laurence, and Kantor, Michael. (2008). *Make 'em Laugh: The Funny Business of America,* Twelve.

Mayo Clinic Staff. (Aug. 6 2014). *Ebola Virus and Marburg Virus Symptoms.*

Mazzulo, Yvonne P. (August 4, 2012). *Fifty Facts You Don't Know About Marilyn Monroe. Examiner.*

McQuillar, Tayannah Lee. Johnson, Fred L. PhD. (January 26, 2010). *Tupac Shakur: The Life and Times of an American Icon.*

NBC Sports. (June 3, 2009). *Tracking Tiger.*

New York Times. (September 7, 1997). *Brother's Eulogy the Very Essence of Compassion.*

Place, Robert. *The Tarot: History, Symbolism and Divination.*

Planas, Antonio. (April 7, 2011). *FBI Outlines Parallels in Notorious B.I.G., Tupac Slayings.* Las Vegas Review-Journal.

Presley, Priscilla. (1985). *Elvis and Me.*

Scorca, Shari. *Bono, Brad Pitt Launch Campaign For Third-World Relief.* MTV News.

Socrates. (430 BC). *Musings.* Athens: Self Published.

Stone, Brad. (October 6, 2011). *Steve Jobs: The Return, 1977 - 2011.*

The Associated Press. (August 30, 2005). *Looters Take Advantage of New Orleans Mess.*

UNHCR. (August 23, 2001) *Angelina Jolie named UNHCR Goodwill Ambassador for refugees.*

Vokes- Dudgeon, Sophie. (August 12, 2014). Us Magazine.

Wikipedia. *Plasma (Physics).*

Wikipedia. *Sharon Stone.*

Woods, Earl, McDaniel, Pete. (1997). *Training a Tiger: Raising a Winner in Golf and in Life.*

## ABOUT THE AUTHOR

Anmarie Uber's interest in the metaphysical field has continued, throughout most of her life. She had her first remembered contact with the other side, at age three, and an insatiable passion, throughout childhood, for ghosts, UFOs and anything paranormal. Anmarie began exploring astrology and numerology at age 16, and tarot, yoga, massage, nutrition, palmistry, crystal healing, Feng Shui, energy healing, and the philosophy of reincarnation at age 21. Her ongoing quest for spiritual truth has been all-consuming, and many times taken precedence over personal needs or worldly goals. Although Anmarie has studied countless spiritual and religious ideologies, she counts "A Course in Miracles" and Gary Renard's book "The Disappearance of the Universe", as having the most profound effect on her life. Anmarie believes in not taking life too seriously, finding the humor in difficult situations, forgiving hardships and lessons with others and having faith. She allows Divine Love to be her guide.

## "Cheat Sheet: How to Name Your Business using Chaldean Numerology"

*Get your FREE COPY here:*

http://anmarieuber.us6.list-

manage1.com/subscribe?u=2ed77f2d2bf9dc54

3d680527b&id=261fc383b4

Printed in September 2018
by Rotomail Italia S.p.A., Vignate (MI) - Italy